❀

Lancelot

❀

Lancelot
The Knight of the Cart

Chrétien de Troyes

Translated from the Old French by
Burton Raffel

Afterword by Joseph J. Duggan

Yale University Press
New Haven & London

Set in Simoncini Garamond type by Tseng Information Systems, Durham, North Carolina. Printed in the United States of America.

Library of Congress Cataloging-in-Publication Data
Chrétien, de Troyes, 12th cent.
[Chevalier de la charrette. English]
Lancelot : the knight of the cart / Chrétien de Troyes : translated from the Old French by Burton Raffel ; afterword by Joseph J. Duggan.
p. cm.
Includes bibliographical references.
ISBN 0-300-07120-5 (cloth : alk. paper). — ISBN 978-0-300-07121-4 (pbk. : alk. paper)
1. Lancelot (Legendary character)—Romances. 2. Romances—Translations into English. 3. Knights and knighthood—Poetry. 4. Arthurian romances.
I. Raffel, Burton. II. Title.
PQ1445.L3E5 1997
841'.1—dc21
97-14424
CIP

A catalogue record for this book is available from the British Library.

The paper in this book meets the guidelines for permanence and durability of the Committee on Production Guidelines for Book Longevity of the Council on Library Resources.

10 9 8 7 6 5 4 3 2 1

To the memory of Francis Patrick Sullivan, S.J.
—who courted life's adventures
with courage, love, and faith

❀

Contents

Translator's Preface

This is the fourth of Chrétien's great narratives I have translated. The first, *Yvain,* was published by Yale University Press in 1987; the second and third, *Erec and Enide* and *Cligès,* were published by Yale in 1997; and after *Lancelot* it is planned to continue and conclude the enterprise with *Perceval: The Story of the Grail.*

Most of what needs to be explained about the technical aspects of this translation has long since been set out, in my Translator's Preface to *Yvain.* And as I also said there, "I will be content if this translation allows the modern reader some reasonably clear view of Chrétien's swift, clear style, his wonderfully inventive story-telling, his perceptive characterizations and sure-handed dialogue, his racy wit and sly irony, and the vividness with which he evokes, for us his twentieth-century audiences, the emotions and values of a flourishing, vibrant world." I need only add that the longer I work with Chrétien, the more "modern" he seems to me, in virtually all his essential characteristics—which may help to explain why, as I said in concluding that prior Translator's Preface, "Chrétien is a delight to read—and to translate." Not easy, but definitely a delight.

Although I have had constantly before me, in all the translations subsequent to *Yvain,* the two most recent editions of the Old French original, the *Oeuvres complètes* (1994), edited for Gallimard's deservedly famous Pléiade series by the late Daniel Poirion and five collaborating scholars, and the complete *Romans* (1994), edited for Le Livre de Poche series, once again, by a team of scholars, I have grown increasingly convinced of the superiority of the Poirion texts. That for *Lancelot, ou le chevalier de la charette,* edited by Poirion, has accordingly been followed in this translation.

Université des Acadiens
Lafayette, Louisiana

❀

Lancelot

Chrétien de Troyes

Puisque ma dame de Chanpaigne
Vialt que romans a feire anpraigne,
Come cil qui est suens antiers
Je l'anprendrai molt volentiers
De quan qu'il puet el monde feire
Sanz rien de losange avant treire

Because my lady of Champagne*
Wants me to start a new
Romance, I'll gladly begin one,
For I'm completely her servant
In whatever she wants me to do,   5
And these are not flattering words.
Others, who like to wheedle
And coax, might start by saying
—And this, too, would not
Be flattery—that here was a princess   10
Who outshines every lady

* Countess Marie de Champagne, oldest daughter of King Louis VII
and Eleanor of Aquitaine

Alive, as the winds of April
And May blow sweetest of all.
But I, by God, refuse
To spin sweet words about 15
My lady. Should I say: "This lady
Is worth her weight in queens,
One gem as good as silks
And onyx?" No, I won't,
But even if I don't, she is. 20
What I have to say is that this
Story has been better polished
By her work and wisdom than by mine.
As Chrétien begins this tale
Of Lancelot, the Knight 25
Of the Cart, he declares that the subject
And its meaning come from his lady.
She gave him the idea, and the story;
His words do the work of her matter.

      And he writes that once, on Ascension 30
Day, King Arthur held court
With all the splendor he loved,
Being so wealthy a king.

      And after dining, Arthur
Remained with his companions, 35
For the hall was full of barons,
And the queen was there, and many
Other beautiful high-born
Ladies, exchanging elegant
Words in the finest French. 40
And Kay, who along with others
Had waited on table, ate
With his stewards. But as he sat down,

A singularly well-equipped knight
Entered, armed to the teeth   45
And armored from head to foot.
Heavily armed as he was,
He walked straight to where
The king was seated among
His barons, but gave him no greeting,   50
Declaring: "Arthur, I hold
Many of your people captive— *prisoners*
Knights, ladies, girls—
But I didn't come here to tell you
I meant to let them go!   55
All I want you to know
Is that neither your wealth nor your strength
Is sufficient to get them back.
Understand me: you'll be sooner
Dead than able to do   60
A thing!" The king answered
That what he couldn't help
He could live with; but it did not make him
Happy. And then their visitor
Started to leave, but got   65
Only as far as the door
Before he turned, stopped,
And instead of descending the steps
Threw back this challenge: "King,
If you have a single knight   70
In this court of yours you can trust
To take your queen to the woods, *Gwen*
Where I'll be going when I'm finished
Here, then I'll agree
To let him have those prisoners   75

I've got in my dungeons, provided
He can defeat me in battle,
It being understood
That possession of your queen is the prize
For victory." Many people   80
In the palace heard him; the court
Was astonished. The news was brought
To Kay, as he sat at his food,
And he rose at once, left
The table, and came to the king,   85
And spoke with bitter anger:
"My lord, I've served you long
And most loyally, and in great
Good faith. But I'm leaving you now,
Never to serve you again.   90
From this moment on, I've not
The slightest desire to serve you."
The king was deeply shocked;
As soon as he found himself
Able to speak, he said,   95
"Is this a joke, or are you
Serious?" "Your majesty,
This is not a time
For joking, but for saying farewell.
I've told you what I want,   100
Nor do I ask for anything
Else: my decision is final,
I intend to leave at once."
"But why is this what you want?"
Asked the king. "Have I given offense?   105
Are you angry? Calm yourself, steward:
Remain at my court. Believe me,

Kay, there's nothing in the world
I wouldn't give to keep
You here, to stop you from leaving."   110
"My lord, we're wasting time.
You couldn't keep me here
With a basket of gold a day."
Deeply upset, Arthur
Hurried to find his queen.   115
"My lady," he said, "you won't
Believe what our steward wants!
He says he's resigning his post
At once—and I don't know why!
He won't listen to me,   120
But perhaps you can change his mind.
So hurry to him, dear lady,
And even if I can't persuade him
He might listen to you.
Throw yourself at his feet!   125
I'll never be happy again
If I lose the pleasures of his presence!"
So the king sent her to seek
The steward, and she went, finding
Kay with a group of knights.   130
Coming directly toward him,
She said: "Kay, let me
Tell you right away,
I come to you deeply troubled
By what I've heard. They say,   135
And it hurts my heart to hear it,
That you wish to leave the king.
What's happened? Why would you do
Such a thing? It's not like you—

Neither courtly nor wise. Please, 140
I beg you: stay with my lord!"
"Lady," he said, "forgive me,
But I can't and I won't." Then the queen
Asked him again, and all
The knights joined in her plea, 145
But Kay assured her she was wasting
Her breath, as they were wasting
Theirs. So the royal lady,
Great as she was, dropped
To her knees and begged him to remain. 150
"Rise, my lady." But she wouldn't,
Swearing she'd stay at his feet
Until he consented. Then Kay
Promised to remain, but only
If Arthur swore in advance 155
He could have whatever he wanted,
And the queen herself agreed.
"Kay," she replied, "whatever
It is, we'll grant it together.
Come: we'll go to the king 160
And tell him your terms." So Kay
And Guinevere went to the king.
"My lord, Kay has agreed
To remain. It wasn't easy
To persuade him. But he said he would stay, 165
Provided you give him what he asks."
The king sighed with pleasure
And said the steward could have
What he wanted, whatever it might be.
"My lord," said Kay, "this 170
Is the gift I want and you

Have pledged yourself to give me.
I'll think myself a fortunate
Man, if you let me have it.
Your queen, who stands beside me,   175
Will be placed under my protection,
And we'll ride off to the woods
In search of the knight and his challenge."
The king was upset, but his word
Had been given, and he could not revoke it,   180
No matter how angry and sorrowful
It made him (which was easy to see).
The queen, too, was deeply
Displeased, and the whole palace
Denounced Kay's pride and presumption   185
In making such a demand.
And then the king took
The queen by the hand, and said,
"Lady, it can't be helped;
You must go with Kay." And the steward   190
Said, "Just trust her to me;
There's nothing to be afraid of.
You can count on me, my lord:
I'll bring her back safe
And sound!" Arthur gave him   195
Her hand, and Kay led her
Out, the entire palace
Following, frowning as they went.
The steward was fully armed,
Of course; his horse stood   200
In the courtyard, waiting, and beside it
The sort of palfrey fit
For a queen to ride, patient,

Calm, not pulling at the bit.
Slowly, the queen approached,   205
And, sighing sadly, mounted,
Then spoke in a voice so soft
No one was meant to hear her:
"Oh, my love, if only
You knew, you'd never let me   210
Take a step in this man's
Care!" It was barely a whisper,
But Count Guinables, who stood
Close by, heard what she'd said.
As they rode toward the woods, everyone   215
Watching, knights and ladies,
Were as sad as if she were being
Buried. They never expected
To see her again, in this life.
And so the steward, impelled   220
By his pride, took her to the woods.
For all their sorrow, none of them
Thought to follow along,
Until Sir Gawain quietly
Said to the king, his uncle,   225
"My lord, I'm quite astonished:
This strikes me as terribly wrong.
If you'll take my advice, as long
As there's time, and they're still in sight,
Let's ride along behind them,   230
You and I and whoever
Joins us. I simply can't keep
Myself from following after:
It makes no sense not to,
At least until we know   235

What happens to the queen, and how well
Kay can take care of her."
"We'll go, good nephew," said the king.
"Yours is a politic wisdom.
And now that you've spoken up,   240
Tell them to bring out our horses
And have them saddled and bridled,
So all we need do is mount."
As soon as the horses were ordered,
They were led out and readied. The king,   245
Of course, was the first to mount,
And then my lord Gawain,
And after him the others.
Everyone wanted to come,
But each in his own way,   250
Some of them armed to the teeth,
Some of them neither armored
Nor carrying weapons. But Gawain
Was fully armed, and had ordered
Two of his squires to bring   255
A pair of battle horses.
And then, as they neared the forest,
They saw Kay's horse, which they knew
At once, come jogging out,
Riderless, and observed that both   260
Its reins had been broken. And as
It approached they saw, too,
That the stirrup-leather was spotted
With blood, and the back of the saddle
Had been broken to bits. It was hardly   265
A pleasant sight; they nodded
And shrugged, knowing what had happened.

My lord Gawain galloped
Far ahead of the others,
Until he saw a knight   270
Come riding slowly toward him
On a tired and heavy-footed
Horse, panting and drenched
With sweat. The knight greeted
My lord Gawain, and Gawain   275
Returned the greeting. And then,
Recognizing Gawain,
The knight stopped and said,
"My lord, I think you can see
What a sweat my horse is in;   280
He's no use at all, in this state.
I believe those horses over
There are yours: may I ask,
Please, that you do me the favor—
Which I'll gladly repay—of either   285
Letting me have, or lending me,
One, whichever you like?"
Said Gawain, "Take your pick:
The one you prefer is yours."
But the knight's need was so pressing   290
He made no attempt to choose
The better, or bigger, or faster,
But simply mounted the one
That happened to be closest, and galloped
Away at once. The horse   295
He left behind him fell dead,
So hard had he been ridden
That day, driven till he dropped.
Without losing a moment,

The knight dashed into   300
The forest, and Gawain followed
As fast as he could, until
He reached the foot of a hill.
Some distance further along
He found the horse the knight   305
Had taken, dead in the road,
And saw the signs of many
Mounted men, and broken
Shields and lances all around.
Clearly, there'd been a furious   310
Fight, involving a good many
Knights, and Gawain was upset
He'd had no part in the battle.
He didn't stop for long,
But rode rapidly ahead   315
Until, suddenly, he saw
The knight, alone and on foot,
In full armor, helmet
On his head, shield around his neck,
Sword at his side. And there   320
Was a cart—used, in those days,
As we use a pillory, now.
In any good-sized town
You'll find them by the thousand, but then
There was only one, and they used it   325
For every kind of criminal,
Exactly like the pillory
Today—murderers, thieves,
Those defeated in judicial
Combat, robbers who roamed   330
In the dark, and those who rode

The highways. Offenders were punished
By being set in the cart
And driven up and down
The town. Their reputations   335
Were lost, and the right to be present
At court; they lost all honor
And joy. Everyone knew
What the carts were for, and feared them;
They'd say, "If you see a cart   340
Coming your way, cross
Yourself, and pray to the Lord
On high, to keep you from evil."
The knight on foot, who had
No lance, came up behind   345
The cart and saw, seated
On the shaft, a dwarf, who like
A carter held a long whip
In his hands. And the knight said,
"Dwarf, in the name of God,   350
Tell me: have you seen my lady
The queen come by?" The dwarf,
Low-born and disgusting, had no
Interest in telling the knight
Anything: "If you feel like taking   355
A ride in this cart of mine,
You might find out, by tomorrow,
What's happened to the queen." The cart
Rolled slowly on, not stopping
For even a moment; and the knight   360
Followed along behind
For several steps, not climbing
Right up. But his hesitant shame

Was wrong. Reason, which warred
With Love, warned him to take care;   365
It taught and advised him never
To attempt anything likely
To bring him shame or reproach.
Reason's rules come
From the mouth, not from the heart.   370
But Love, speaking from deep
In the heart, hurriedly ordered him
Into the cart. He listened
To Love, and quickly jumped in,
Putting all sense of shame   375
Aside, as Love had commanded.
Then my lord Gawain came galloping
Up, chasing the cart,
And seeing the knight seated
Inside it could not keep from gaping,   380
And said, "Dwarf, give me
News of the queen, if you have any."
The dwarf answered, "If you loathe
Yourself, as this other knight does,
Climb up and sit beside him,   385
And I'll take you both at once."
This struck my lord Gawain
As the height of absolute folly,
And he said he wouldn't climb in,
Not caring to exchange his horse   390
For a dirty criminal's cart.
"Just go wherever you're going,"
He said, "and I'll follow along."
        So off they went, one
On his horse, two in the cart,   395

But all traveling the same
Road. That evening they came
To a castle—and what a beautiful,
Noble place it was!
They entered through a gate,   400
And the people inside were astonished
By the sight of a knight in a cart,
But felt no quiet compassion:
High-born or low, young or
Old, they hooted and cried   405
Up and down the streets,
And the knight could hear them saying
Disgusting things, all of them
Wondering: "What will happen
To this knight? Is he ready to be roasted?   410
Flayed or hanged? Will they drown him,
Or burn him on a brushwood fire?
Tell us, driver, dwarf!
What did they catch him doing?
Is he just a thief? Or maybe   415
A murderer? Was he beaten in combat?"
No one received an answer;
The dwarf ignored them all.
With Gawain riding behind him,
He drove the knight to his lodgings—   420
A tower standing in the open
Fields, right in front of
The town, a meadow to one side,
And then a ridge of grayish
Rock, on which the tower   425
Was set, straight and tall.
The cart rolled in, and Gawain

Came riding after. In the great
Hall of this lovely building
He was greeted by a beautiful lady,   430
The fairest in that whole country,
And with her came a pair
Of well-born, gracious girls.
As soon as they saw Gawain
They clapped their hands in delight,   435
And after making him welcome
Began asking questions:
"Tell us, dwarf: what
Did he do, this knight in your cart?"
The dwarf refused to answer,   440
But ordered the knight out
Of the cart, then disappeared;
And no one knew where he went.
My lord Gawain dismounted;
Two young pages appeared,   445
And helped the knights disarm.
Others brought fur-lined cloaks,
And both knights put them on.
When dinnertime came, the table
Was bountifully set. My lord   450
Gawain and the lady were seated
Side by side. Neither
Knight needed different
Or better lodgings: all through
The evening the lady honored   455
Them both with her noble, elegant
Company and her gracious manners.
        Once they had eaten their fill,
A pair of immense beds

Were readied, side by side   460
In the middle of the hall, and then
A third, richer and finer
Than either of the others: according
To the story, no one has ever
Imagined such a splendid bed,   465
Delightfully designed and furnished.
And when it was time to sleep
The lady took her guests
To where these beds had been readied.
She showed them the first two   470
And explained, "These are for you.
But that one's reserved for those
Who deserve such splendor: it's not
For you to sleep in." And the knight
Who'd come to that tower riding   475
In a cart, with a dwarf as his driver,
Replied to this prohibition
With utter contempt and disdain:
"And why," he demanded, "is this bed
Forbidden?" The lady's answer   480
Was ready and waiting; she needed
No pause for thought or reflection:
"It's not for you," she declared,
"To demand such things. Any
Knight who's ridden in a cart   485
Has lost his honor forever.
You have no right to ask
Such questions and expect to be answered—
And certainly not to sleep
In that bed. You'll pay dearly,   490
If you do! I never prepared

So rich a place for the likes
Of you. Don't even think of it."
"You'll be seeing me there," he said.
"Oh, really?" "Indeed." "Then do   495
As you please." "Whatever it costs,"
Said the knight, "whoever's annoyed,
Whoever gets hurt, by God!
I haven't the faintest idea.
But I'll be sleeping in this bed   500
Tonight, and sleeping well."
    The bed was almost a yard
Longer than the others, and as soon
As his armor was off he stretched himself
Out on the yellow satin,   505
Embroidered with gold. That bed
Hadn't been lined with wornout
Squirrel pelts but with deep,
Thick sable, worthy of warming
A king. The mattress he lay on   510
Wasn't mere hay or reeds
Or old straw mats! And then,
At midnight, hurled like lightning,
A spear came crashing across   *bed test #1*
The bed, point first, so close   515
To the sleeping knight that it almost
Pinned him between the ribs,
Stitched him to the blanket and the white
Sheets. And that spear bore
A burning pennant, and the blanket   520
And sheets began to flame,
And the whole bed was on fire.
But though the point passed

So near the knight that it drew
A faint line across   525
His skin, it did not wound him.
The knight sat up, beat out
The flames, took the spear,
And threw it to the middle of the hall,
And—never leaving the bed—   530
Lay down once more and slept
As calm and restful a sleep
As before, peaceful and at ease.
　　　　Early next morning, having
Ordered a Mass for her guests,   535
The lady who lived in the tower
Came to call them from their beds.
Once Mass had been sung,
The knight who'd ridden in the cart
Walked, deep in thought,   540
To a window opening out
On the meadows, and stood looking
Across the fields. At the very
Next window the young lady of the tower
Was discussing something (I've no idea   545
What) for a moment, with my lord
Gawain; no one could hear
What they said. But while they were leaning
And looking, they saw a corpse,
The body of a dead knight,   550
Being carried down from the meadows
And along the river, and beside him,
Weeping and wailing, came
Three ladies, mourning as they went.
A great procession followed   555

The bier, preceded by a noble
Knight, leading at his left
Hand a beautiful lady.
The knight at the window knew her
At once: this was the queen,   560
And his eyes followed her along
The path, watching with passionate
Care, thrilled at the sight,
For as long as he could. Then,
When he wasn't able to see her,   565
His body went slack, he felt
He could let himself fall from the window, !
And was halfway over the sill
When Gawain saw him and, from
Behind, pulled him back,   570
Saying, "Be calm, my lord:
In the name of God, don't even
Think of committing such folly!
How wrong to despise your life!"
"He's right to despise it," said the lady.   575
"Do you think there's anyone who hasn't
Heard what happened? Of course
He'd rather be dead, now
That he's ridden in the cart. For him,
Death would be better than life,   580
For all life holds is shame,
Contempt, and misery." Both knights
Asked for their armor and weapons,
And made themselves ready. And the lady
Displayed a noble politeness: 585
Having jeered and mocked more
Than enough, now she gave

The knight, as a mark of affection
And respect, a horse and a spear.
And the knights left her like civilized   590
Men, well trained in courtesy,
Bowing and wishing her well,
Then riding away, following
After the procession they'd seen.
No one could exchange a word   595
With either knight, they galloped
So fast. They rode hard
Down the road the queen had taken,
But couldn't catch the funeral
Party, which had hurried off.   600
Leaving the fields, they crossed
A fence and found a well-kept
Road, which led them across
A forest. It was early morning
When they came to a crossroads and saw   605
A girl, whom they both greeted,
Asking, with careful courtesy,
If by any chance she knew,
And was able to tell them, where
The queen had been taken. She answered   610
Soberly, saying, "Offer
Me enough and, yes,
I can certainly tell you. I can set you
On the right road, and name you
The land they've gone to and the knight   615
Who's led them there. But you'll need
To be ready for immense hardships,
If you try to follow them! It takes
Pain and suffering to get there."

My lord Gawain replied, 620
"With God's good help, my lady,
I pledge myself and whatever
Strength I have to your service,
Whenever you need me, if only
You'll tell me the truth." The knight *becomes his* 625
Who'd ridden in the cart offered *name*
More than all his strength,
Swearing, with all the force
And power that Love had given him,
That nothing would stand in his way 630
And, fearing nothing, he'd come
Whenever she called and do
Whatever she wanted done.
"You'll hear it all!" she cried,
And immediately began her tale: 635
        "On my faith, lords, a most powerful
Knight, Méléagant,
Son of the king of Gorre,
Has taken the queen to that land
No one visits and ever 640
Returns, forced to remain
In exile, serving that lord."
Then the knight of the cart demanded:
"Where can we find that land,
Lady? How do we get there?" 645
She answered, "I'll certainly tell you.
But understand: you'll meet
With many obstacles, and many
Dangers; it won't be easy,
Without the king's permission. 650
His name is Bademaguz.

But two desperately dangerous
Bridges can get you in.
One is called THE SUNKEN
BRIDGE—because, in fact,   655
It's under the water, exactly
Halfway down, set
Right in the middle, as much
Water below as above it,
Hung between surface and bottom.   660
And since it's barely a foot
And a half in width and thickness,
It's a feast you ought to refuse—
Though it's far and away the least
Dangerous. (There are many other   665
Pathways I won't even mention.)
But the second bridge is the worst,
So exceedingly risky that no one
Has ever gotten across,
For it's honed as sharp as a sword blade—   670
Which is why it's called THE SWORD
BRIDGE. Whatever I've told you
Is true, and as much of the truth
As it's in my power to tell you."
At which they asked: "Lady,   675
Would you like to explain how
We can get to each of these bridges?"
And the girl answered, "Right
Over there is a straight road
To the Sunken Bridge; the other   680
Will lead you to the Sword Bridge."
And then the knight who'd ridden
In the cart said to his companion,

"Sir, it's up to you:
Pick whichever route   685
You prefer; I'll take the other.
Choose whichever you like."
"By God," said my lord Gawain,
"It isn't much of a choice;
They're both wickedly dangerous.   690
I know no way to decide
Between them. Which would be better?
But how can I hesitate,
Since you've given me the choice?
I'll go to the Sunken Bridge."   695
"Then we're agreed. There's nothing
More to be said. You take
Your road, and I'll take mine."
And then the three of them went
In their different directions, warmly   700
Commending each other to God.
But just as she turned to leave them,
The girl said, "Remember:
You both owe me whatever
Reward I want, whenever   705
I want it. Don't forget."
"Indeed we won't, my dear,"
The knights answered as one.
And so they took their leave.
Mind and body, the knight   710
Of the cart remained in Love's
Firm grip, helpless against it;
His thoughts were so tumbled about
That he no longer knew who he was,
Or if he truly existed,   715

Or what his name might be,
Or whether he was wearing armor,
Or where he was going or from where
He'd come. All he could think of
Was one woman, for whom   720
He'd forgotten everything else—
And he thought of her so intently
That he heard and saw and knew
Nothing. But his horse galloped
Ahead, on all the right roads,   725
The most direct paths,
And as luck would have it brought
His master to an open place
Near a river crossing.
The other side of the ford   730
Was guarded by an armed knight,
Accompanied by a girl who rode
A peaceful palfrey. The sun
Was already starting down,
But our love-stricken knight had never   735
Left his silent dreamworld.
His horse, which was terribly thirsty,
Saw the bright, clear water,
And headed directly toward it.
The sentinel on the other side   740
Shouted: "Knight! I guard
This ford. You're forbidden to cross."
Our knight neither listened nor heard,
Lost in the whirling thoughts
That never left him; his horse   745
Hurried straight to the water.
The sentinel called out again:

"Leave, if you know what's good for you.
You can't cross here."
And he swore by the heart in his chest   750
He'd attack, if our knight came further.
And still his words went unheard.
So he cried, one final time:
"Knight! Stay out of the ford.
It's forbidden, I've already told you.   755
I swear by the head on my shoulders
I'll attack the moment you try it."
But all our knight heard was his own
Thoughts. His horse leapt
Straight from the bank to the water,   760
And drank as fast as he could.
The sentinel swore to make
Our knight pay: no shield would protect him,
Nor would the mail shirt he wore.
He spurred his horse to a gallop,   765
Then whipped it to its fastest pace,
And struck our knight so fiercely
That he stretched him out in the water
No one was allowed to cross.
His spear, too, fell   770
In the water, and the shield from around
His neck. But the water woke him:
Blinking, at best half-conscious,
Like someone just out of bed,
He jumped to his feet, astonished   775
To find himself where he was.
And then he saw the sentinel,
And shouted, "You! Why
Did you hit me? Explain yourself,

For I never knew you were there,   780
And I've done nothing to harm you."
"You did, by God," was the answer.
"Didn't you treat me like dirt
When I told you, three times over,
And as loud and clear as I could,   785
That you couldn't cross? You had
To hear me, at least the second
Time, or the third, but you rode
Right on, although I warned you
I'd strike if you entered that water."   790
But our knight immediately answered,
"As far as I'm concerned,
I never saw you and I never
Heard you! Maybe you did
Forbid me to cross. But I   795
Was lost in my thoughts. Believe me,
Just let me get my hands
On your bridle, and you'll regret it!"
"Oh, really?" the sentinel answered.
"And what will you do? Come over   800
Here and hang on my bridle,
If you're brave enough to try it.
All your boasting and threats
Aren't worth a fistful of ashes."
"There's nothing I'd like better,"   805
Our knight answered. "You'll see
Exactly what happens as soon as
I get my hands on you."
And then our knight waded
To the middle of the stream, and grasped   810
The sentinel's reins in his left

Hand, and seized his leg
With the right, pulling and twisting
So hard that the other cried out
In pain: he felt as if   815
His leg was about to be pulled
From his body, and begged our knight
To stop, saying, "Knight,
If you'd like to challenge me, man
To man, go get your horse,   820
And your shield, and your spear, and I'll gladly
Fight you." "By God, I won't
Let go," said our knight. "I'm afraid
You'll run away the minute
You're free." Deeply shamed,   825
The sentinel said, "Knight,
You can mount your horse in peace.
I promise I'll neither trick you
Nor run away. You've shamed me,
And now I'm angry." But our knight   830
Only replied, "Not
Till you've solemnly sworn you won't
Play tricks, or run, or ride
Toward me, or touch me, until
You see me mounted. I'd do you   835
A great favor, if I set you
Free, now that I've got you."
And so he swore, for he had to.
As soon as he had the sentinel's
Solemn word, our knight   840
Went to collect his shield
And spear, which had floated far
From the ford, carried by the swift

so distracted, he's neglecting his knightly duties/position

Current. Then he returned
And took possession of his horse.   845
And when he was back in the saddle
He hung the shield around
His neck, and set his spear
Against the saddle bow.
And then the knights ran   850
At one another as fast
As their horses could gallop. The sentinel
Struck the very first blow,
Striking so hard that his spear
Shattered. Then a blow from our knight   855
Drove him off his horse,
Deep down in the water.
And our knight leapt from his horse,
Sure he could drive in front of him
At least a hundred such enemies.   860
He drew his great steel sword
Just as the sentinel, leaping
Up, drew his, gleaming
Bright, and they fought once more,
Holding their shining shields   865
In front of them, protecting themselves,
For both sharp blades were busy,
Always moving, never
At rest. They beat at each other,
Relentless, the fighting so furious   870
That our knight began to feel,
Deep in his heart, ashamed
To be at it so long, working
So hard to finish what he'd started,
And wondering if he'd ever succeed   875

In his mission, if a single knight
Could delay him. It seemed to him
That, just the day before,
If he'd met a hundred such knights
In a valley, he'd have beaten them all   880
By now; he was anxious, and worried,
Finding himself forced
To waste his time, and so many
Blows. He attacked the sentinel
So fiercely that he turned and ran,   885
Reluctantly giving up
Control of the ford. But our knight
Was not done: he chased the other
Down, and drove him to the ground
On all fours, swearing as he swung   890
His sword he'd soon regret
Tumbling a traveler in the stream
And interrupting his thoughts.
The girl who'd come with the sentinel
Heard these fearsome threats   895
And, much afraid, begged
Our knight not to kill him.
But the knight of the cart informed her
He couldn't show mercy to someone
Who'd made him suffer such shame.   900
So our knight came forward, sword
Raised, and the sentinel cried,
"For the sake of God, and for me,
Grant me the mercy I asked for!"
Our knight answered, "May God   905
Love me, I've never denied
Mercy to a man who did me

Wrong, if he asked in God's name.
I'll grant you mercy, this once,
For His sake. It's only right: 910
I can't refuse you, when you ask
Not in your own name, but His.
But first, swear in His name
You'll remain my prisoner, and come
Whenever I call you." The oath   915
Was a hard one, but the sentinel swore it.
And then the girl spoke
Again, "Knight, if you please,
Now that he's begged for mercy
And you have agreed to grant it,   920
If ever before you've freed
A captive, release this one
To me; let me have him
In return for my pledge to grant you
Whatever you want, whenever   925
You ask it, if I possibly can."
Hearing her words, the knight
Of the cart knew who she was,
And immediately freed his prisoner.
But knowing that he knew her caused   930
The girl immense anguish:
It was exactly what she did not want.
So she hurried them off on their way,
She and the sentinel commending
Our knight to God, and requesting   935
His permission to leave. It was granted.
Then the knight of the cart rode on
Until it was almost evening,
When he saw a beautiful girl,

Elegantly dressed and bejeweled.   940
She greeted him with courteous,
Well-bred words, and our knight
Answered, "May God grant you
Good health and happiness."
She said, "Sir, my house   945
Is nearby, ready to receive you
If you decide to use it.
But in order to enjoy my home
You have to sleep with me.
My offer's conditional and these   950
Are my terms." Many men
Would have thanked her a thousand times over,
But our knight's face went dark
And his answer was very different:
"I thank you, lady, for the offer   955
Of your home, which is gracious and welcome,
But as far as sleeping's concerned,
With your kind permission, I'll decline."
"By God, you'll get nothing,"
Said the girl, "unless you agree."   960
And seeing he had no choice,
Our knight accepted her offer,
Though it gave him pain to say so—
But that was nothing, compared
To what he'd suffer that night!   965
And the girl who took him to bed
Would experience trouble and shame—
Or perhaps she'd love him so much
She wouldn't want to let him
Leave her. Once he'd consented,   970
Agreed to do as she wished,

She led him to a castle courtyard
Finer than any in Thessaly,
Surrounded on all sides
By high walls and a deep
Moat. But the only man   975
In that place was the one she'd brought there.
      She'd had a suite of beautiful
Rooms readied, and a huge,
Stately hall. They'd reached   980
Her home, after riding along
Beside a river, and the drawbridge
Had been lowered, well in advance,
To allow them to cross. They rode
Over the bridge, and found   985
The castle hall open;
It was covered by a tiled roof.
The gate, too, was open,
And inside they saw a round
Table on which a great cloth   990
Had been spread, and plates had been brought,
And burning candles glowed
In their appointed places; there were gold-
Plated silver cups,
And a pair of bowls, one full   995
Of blackberry wine, the other
Of good strong white. Two basins
Of warm water, for washing
Their hands, had been set at one end
Of a bench, and at the other   1000
A handsome towel, brightly
Worked, for drying themselves.
But not a single servant

Or steward or waiter could be seen.
The knight of the cart lifted   1005
His shield from his neck and hung it
From a hook, and set his spear
In a rack, high on the wall.
Then he dismounted, and the lady,
Too, came down from her saddle.   1010
And he was grateful, seeing
How she chose not
To wait for his help. As soon
As her feet had touched the ground,
Not hesitating a moment,   1015
She ran inside, to a room
From which she brought a scarlet
Cloak for him to wear.
The room was bright, as though the night
Sky was filled with stars;   1020
So many candles were burning,
So many flaring torches,
It was almost like daylight. Once
She'd draped the cloak around
His shoulders, she said, "My friend,   1025
This basin of water, and this towel,
Are for you to use: there's no one
Here to help you. You
And I are alone, as you see.
So wash your hands, if you like,   1030
Then seat yourself wherever
You please, and—since it's time
For eating—eat what you will."
"Gladly." So he washed his hands
And sat where he pleased, and she came   1035

And sat beside him, and they ate
And drank together. And then
It was time to leave the table.
          And as soon as they rose, the girl
Said to the knight, "My lord,   1040
Try the night air for a bit,
If you wouldn't mind, and if
You please, linger a while,
Until you think I've been able
To put myself to bed.   1045
Don't be offended or displeased,
For then you can honor your promise."
"You have my word," he replied,
"That I'll be in your bed as soon
As I think the hour has come."   1050
Then he walked outside, staying
In the courtyard for a long while,
Until it was time to return,
For he needed to honor his pledge.
But coming back to the hall   1055
He could not find the girl
Who wanted to be his lover.
He searched, but could not see her,
And said to himself, "Wherever
She's gone, I'll go and find her."   1060
He set out at once, determined
To keep his word. And just
As he started toward the other
Rooms, he heard a girl
Screaming, and knew the voice   1065
For the girl he was supposed to sleep with.
Seeing an open door,

He went in that direction
And saw, right in front of him,
A knight who had tumbled the girl,   1070
Her clothes turned up, across
A bed, and was holding her down.
And she, thinking surely
He'd come to help her, cried
As loud as she could, "Help me,   1075
Help me! Knight! My guest!
Unless you get him off me
He'll dishonor me while you watch!
You're the one I'm supposed
To sleep with—you promised! Can you let him   1080
Take me like this, by force,
Right under your eyes?
Oh noble knight, please!
Hurry, help me, before
It's too late!" The girl was almost   1085
Naked, and the knight was shamelessly
Pushing her down, and our knight
Felt deeply humiliated,
Seeing their bodies one
On the other; he felt no desire   1090
And not the slightest jealousy.
But the door was guarded by a pair
Of knights, both well armed,
Their swords already drawn.
And inside the room were four   1095
Men at arms, each
With an ax sharp enough
To cut an ox in half
As easily as chopping roots

And branches from reeds and bushes.   1100
Our knight stood where he was,
Uncertain: "My God, what
Can I do? I began this great
Quest for Guinevere's sake.
I can't proceed if my heart   1105
Is only as brave as a rabbit's:
If Cowardice lends me its strength,
And I march at its command,
I'll never achieve my goal.
To stay right here would be shameful—   1110
And even thinking such thoughts
Brings me dishonor. My heart
Would be black and worthless: by God,
It makes me miserable to have waited
This long, it's a mortal shame   1115
To have lingered here like this.
How can I hope for God's
Mercy if I'm driven by pride?
If I don't prefer an honorable
Death to a life of shame?   1120
What honor could I possibly gain,
If the door had been left unguarded?
If these fellows stepped back and let me
Go in unchallenged? By God,
The lowest man among men   1125
Could accomplish all that! I hear
That miserable creature calling
For help, over and over,
In the name of the promise I made her,
And cursing me for not coming."   1130
He approached the door, risking

His head and his neck for a quick
Look up at the guards,
And saw the swords coming
At him. So he pulled back his head,   1135
And the knights, unable to stop
Their stroke, swung so savagely
Hard that both swords struck
The ground and shattered. And seeing them
Smashed to pieces, he worried   1140
A good deal less about
Those axes waiting inside.
He jumped inside, struck
One man at arms, and then
Another, the first he could get to,   1145
Clubbing them with elbows and fists
And stretching them out on the ground.
The third one swung, and missed;
The fourth one sliced his cloak,
And his shirt, and cut through   1150
To the white flesh of his shoulder,
Which quickly began to bleed.
Our knight paid no attention
To his wound, leaping swiftly
Across the room and grasping   1155
By the head the man who was trying
To force the girl. Our knight
Meant to honor his promise,
Before he was done! Like it
Or not, he yanked the head back.   1160
But the fellow who'd missed him, at first,
Came rushing over as fast
As he could, raising his ax,

Planning to split our knight's skull
Down to the teeth. Knowing   1165
How to defend himself,
Our knight dragged the rapist
In front of the blow, which fell
Right between the neck
And the shoulder, and cut them apart.   1170
And then our knight took hold of
The ax and quickly wrenched it
Out of the fellow's hands,
Then dropped the man he'd been holding,
Needing to defend himself   1175
Against the two remaining
Knights and the men at arms
With axes, who had launched a savage
Attack. Leaping between
The bed and the wall, he called: 1180
"Come on, all of you! Now
That I've got an ax, and space
To swing it, you couldn't beat me
Even with another twenty
Or thirty to help you!" And then   1185
The girl, who'd been watching, said,
"By God, knight, you've nothing
To fear, with me at your side!"
With a snap of the wrist, she waved
Away knights and men   1190
And all. And at once, without
A word of protest, they left.
And then the girl added,
"My lord, how well you've held off
My entire household! Now come   1195

With me; I'll show you the way."
Holding his hand, she led him
Back to the great hall.
He followed along, unhappy.
    A bed stood ready in the middle   1200
Of the hall, beautifully made
With soft, flowing white sheets—
No flat straw mattress for them,
No rough and wrinkled blankets!
A coverlet of flowered   1205
Silk, double thickness,
Had been spread on top, and the girl,
Still wearing her chemise,
Lay on it. How hard it was
For him, taking off   1210
His shoes and undressing! He was sweating
Freely, but even suffering
As he was, he meant to honor
His pledge. Was he being forced?
Almost: he was forcing himself   1215
To sleep with the girl; his promise
Called him, and bent his will.
He lay on the bed, slowly,
Carefully, like her still wearing
His shirt, so cautious as he stretched   1220
Out on his back that no part
Of his body was touching hers.
Nor did he say a word—
As if he'd been a monk,
Forbidden to speak in his bed.   1225
He stared at the ceiling, seeing
Neither her nor anything

Else. He could not pretend
Goodwill. And why? His heart
Had been captured by another woman,   1230
And even a beautiful face
Cannot appeal to everyone.
The only heart our knight
Owned was no longer his
To command, having already   1235
Been given away; there was nothing
Left. Love, which rules
All hearts, allows them only
One home. "All hearts?" No:
All that Love finds worthy,   1240
Love's approval being worth
A great deal. And Love valued
Our knight higher than any,
Creating such pride in his heart
That I cannot blame him, and I will not,   1245
For renouncing what Love denied him
And striving for the love Love meant him
To have. The girl could see
Her company caused him discomfort;
He'd gladly have let her go,   1250
Clearly determined not
To touch her or seek her favor.
So she said, "With your permission,
My lord, I think I'll leave you,
And sleep in my own bed;   1255
You'll be more at your ease, alone.
I can't believe you find me
Delightful, or ever will.
Don't think me crude, please,

For speaking my mind so plainly.   1260
You're entitled to a good night's sleep,
Having so completely
Carried out your pledge
That there's nothing more I can ask.
Let me commend you to God.   1265
And now I'll go." She left him,
Which caused him no grief at all;
He was pleased to let her leave,
For his heart was fully committed
To someone else. The girl   1270
Saw and understood
His relief. She sought her own bed,
Undressed and lay herself down,
And then she said to herself,
"Of all the knights I've ever   1275
Known, none have been worth
A penny—half a penny!—
Except for him. And I know
Exactly why: he's set
His heart on a quest so grand,   1280
So painful, so full of danger,
That no other knight could attempt it.
May God grant him success!"
And then she fell asleep,
And lay in her bed till dawn.   1285
        But she woke, and hurriedly rose,
At the very first light of morning.
The knight was awake, too;
He dressed and put on his armor,
Waiting for no one's help.   1290
Coming to the hall, she saw

He was ready, and said, as soon
As she joined him, "Knight, may this day
Go well for you." "May it
Go well for you, my lady,"   1295
He answered at once, adding
He was anxious to have his horse
Brought out with no further delay.
She led him into the courtyard,
Saying, "My lord, I'll join you   1300
For much of this journey, if you think
You're able to safely escort me
Along the road, according
To our ancient rules and customs,
Here in the kingdom of Logres."   1305
Which customs were, in those days,
That a knight finding a lady
Or a girl, alone and unguarded,
Should sooner cut his own throat
Than do her the slightest harm   1310
Or offer even the faintest
Thought of any dishonor,
If he meant to preserve his good name,
For if he shamed the young woman
He'd be banished from every court   1315
In the world. But when a knight
Was her escort, that knight could be challenged—
And should he be beaten in battle,
Conquered by force of arms,
The winner, without any shadow   1320
Of disgrace, could do as he liked
With the woman. Which is why the girl
Had asked him if he dared take her

In hand, and lead her about,
According to these rules, which no one   1325
Could ignore while he was with her.
And the knight of the cart answered,
"I guarantee no one
Will hurt you unless they hurt me
First." "In which case, I'll come."   1330
She ordered her palfrey saddled,
And so it was, at once,
And led right out, along
With the knight's horse. They mounted
Without a squire to help,   1335
And then they galloped off.
She tried talking, but he had, *ouch*
No interest in her words and neither
Heard them nor replied: he reveled
In his thoughts, but speech was painful.   1340
Love kept scratching open
The wounds he'd suffered for Love.
He'd never bothered to bandage them
Over, or tried to heal them:
From the moment he'd felt the blow   1345
And known he was hurt, he'd never
Longed for relief or sought
To be cured but, grateful, hungered
For his pain.
            They followed the road
Wherever it led them, and at last   1350
Came to a flowing spring,
Emerging from the middle of a meadow.
A great rock stood
Beside it, and lying on that stone,

Left by God knows who,   1355
Was a comb of ivory and gold.
Since the days of the giant Ysoré
No one, wise man or fool,
Had seen its like. And half
A handful of hair had been left there   1360
By whoever had used it last.
       The girl saw the spring
And the stone, and thought it better
That the knight of the cart did not,
So she turned down another road.   1365
And he was so lost in his thoughts,
And all their pleasures, that at first
He paid no attention, but let her
Lead him out of the path,
Yet when he finally noticed   1370
He was afraid of being tricked,
Sure she had swerved away
From the road to keep from encountering
Something dangerous. "Stop,
Young lady. This is the wrong   1375
Road. We need to go that way.
One never finds the way
By leaving the right road."
"My lord," said the girl, "this one
Is better. I know the way."   1380
He answered, "I've no idea,
Lady, what's in your mind,
But clearly this road's the one
Everyone's followed. Just look.
You can't turn me aside   1385
And start me in some other direction.

Go back, if you like, or come
With me down the road we've been riding."
So on they went, and soon
He saw the stone, and the comb.   1390
"My lord!" he exclaimed. "Never
In all my life have I seen
Such a comb!" "Fetch it for me,"
Said the girl. "Gladly," he said,
And bent, and picked it up.   1395
And then he held it, staring
At the strands of hair it held,
Until the girl began
To laugh. And the knight of the cart
Asked her why she was laughing.   1400
"Just be quiet," she said.
"I won't tell you, right now."
"Why not?" "I don't feel like talking."
Hearing this, he begged her
In the name of her lover, if she had one,   1405
To tell him, for lovers should never
Lie or conceal the truth.
"If there's anyone you love,
Lady, with all your heart,
Let me ask and plead and demand   1410
In his name that you tell me the truth."
"Who could deny such
A request?" she said. "I'll tell you
Whatever I know, and tell you
Truly. Unless I'm mistaken   1415
I recognize this comb.
It belongs to the queen, I know
It does. And these hairs that you see,

So bright, so clear, so brilliant,
Left in the teeth of this comb,   1420
They come from the queen's head:
No other field could have grown them."
And the knight replied, "By God,
The world is full of kings
And queens. Which one do you mean?"   1425
She answered, "Good lord, your lordship!
King Arthur's queen, of course."
Brave as he was, he almost
Fell from his horse, hearing
These words; he supported himself   1430
By leaning down as hard
As he could against the bow
Of his saddle. The girl was astonished,
Stunned by this sudden reaction
And truly afraid he might fall.   1435
And who could blame her, for he seemed
Unconscious, lost to his senses,
And very nearly was,
As close as a man can come,
For his heart was filled with such sadness   1440
That for a long moment the blood
In his face disappeared, and his mouth
Could not move. The girl slipped
From her horse and ran to his side
As fast as she could, to hold   1445
Him up and keep him from falling—
The very last thing in the world
She wanted! But seeing her come
He was shamed, and demanded, "Why
Are you here? It's none of your business."   1450

emasculated

Don't think the girl was stupid
Enough to tell him the truth
And shame him still more: she saw
What pain it would cause him, knowing
She'd seen his weakness. Guarding   1455
Her tongue, she said, simply,
In her best and most courteous manner,
"My lord, I came for that comb:
That's all I want—and I want it
So badly I'll never be happy   1460
Until I get it!" He was willing
To hand it over, but first
He gently removed the queen's
Hair, not breaking a single
Strand. Once a man   1465
Has fallen in love with a woman
No one in all the world
Can lavish such wild adoration
Even on the objects she owns,
Touching them a hundred thousand   1470
Times, caressing with his eyes,
His lips, his forehead, his face.
And all of it brings him happiness,
Fills him with the richest delight;
He presses it into his breast,   1475
Slips it between his shirt
And his heart—worth more than a wagon-
Load of emeralds or diamonds,
Holy relics that free him
Of disease and infection: no powdered   1480
Pearls and ground-up horn
And snail shells for him! No prayers

she doesn't want to embarass him

To Saints Martin and James: his faith
In her hair is complete, he needs
No more. And their real power?   1485
You'd take me for a liar, and a fool,
If I told you the truth—if they offered him
Everything displayed at the Fair
Of Saint-Denis he wouldn't
Have exchanged the hairs he'd found   1490
For the whole bursting lot of it.
And if you're still hunting
The truth, let me tell you that gold
Refined a hundred times,
And then again, would have seemed   1495
To him, if you set that gold
Against a single strand
Of hair, darker than night
Compared to a summer's day.
But I need to get on with my story.   1500
The girl carried off
The comb, and quickly remounted,
While he was ravished with delight   *erotic*
By what he bore above
His heart. Then they crossed the plain   1505
And entered a forest so dense
That riding side by side
Became impossible, and they went
In single file, one
Behind the other, the girl   1510
In front, spurring her horse
Forward in a straight line.
Just as the path narrowed
Still further, they saw a man

Approaching, and even at a distance   1515
The girl immediately knew
Who he was, and said, "Sir knight,
Do you see that man riding
Toward us, fully armed
And armored, and ready for battle?   1520
He thinks he's going to take me
Away, without resistance:
I know him, I know what he's thinking.
He loves me with a wild passion,
And for a very long time he's begged   1525
For my love, and sent me messages,
But I'll never love him, it's out
Of the question, completely impossible.
In the name of God, I'd rather
Be dead than his lover! Right   1530
This minute, I know it, he's as thrilled
At the thought of having me as if
I were lying in his arms. And now
We'll see what you're able to do,
We'll learn if you're truly brave: *another test*   1535
The time has come. Can you really
Protect me, as you said you could?
Can a woman rely on your word?
I'll be able to tell the world,
For better or worse, just what   1540
You're made of." He answered, "Fine,
Fine," and seemed to be saying,
"How can you worry? You're frightening
Yourself for nothing. Why
Be afraid, as long as I'm here?"   1545
        While they spoke, the approaching

Knight, wasting no time,
Came whipping his horse at a furious
Gallop, dashing straight at them,
Hurrying hard to keep   1550
From wasting such a wonderful chance,
Delighted to see this woman
He loved. He saluted her warmly:
"You I've longed for so long,
From whom I've had so little   1555
Joy and so much suffering,
Welcome, wherever you've come from!"
How rude she'd have been, not
To reply at all. She returned
Words that acknowledged his presence,   1560
And though they were only words,
And meant nothing, he was thrilled
To hear even so formal
A greeting as the girl gave him,
Though the mere speaking neither   1565
Stained her lips nor cost her
Much of an effort. He couldn't
Have been more pleased, right then,
Had he fought and won in a splendid
Tournament; no honor, no glory,   1570
Would have meant so much. And thinking
So well of himself, he reached out
His hand and seized her palfrey's
Reins: "Now I've got you!
How well my heart has steered me,   1575
Bringing me home to this port!
All my troubles are over!
At the end of danger there's safety;

At the end of torment there's delight;
At the end of sickness there's health.   1580
Everything I've wanted is mine—
To think of finding you
Like this! I can take you for my own
And no one can call me to account!"
"You're wasting your breath," she said.   1585
"I'm under this knight's protection."
"He's no protection at all:
I'm taking you right now—
And this knight of yours would sooner
Swallow a sack of salt   1590
Than risk a fight with me! *ha!*
The man who can keep me away
From you has yet to be born.
I'll lead you away while he watches,
Without any trouble, whether   1595
He likes it or not. Let him
Try to stop me, if he dares!"
The knight of the cart replied
Calmly, paying no
Attention to this loud boasting,   1600
But quietly, clearly disputing
The claim: "Not so fast, my friend.
Don't waste so many words;
Speak with a bit of balance.
I've no intention of depriving   1605
You of your rights, once
You have them. But understand:
This girl is under my
Protection. Release her: you've held on
Too long. You're forbidden to harm her."   1610

But the other would rather have been burned
Alive than lose his catch!
"It wouldn't be right," said our knight,
"To let you lead her away.
You'll have to fight me first.   1615
But if you're really prepared
For combat, we'll have to find
Some better place than this narrow
Path.—some open road,
Perhaps, or a meadow, or a field."   1620
The other wanted nothing
More: "I agree, of course.
You're quite right; this road
Is far too narrow. My horse
Is already squeezed so tight   1625
I doubt he could turn around
Without breaking his leg."
But though it was hard, he managed
To turn, somehow not hurting
Either the animal or himself,   1630
Then said, "What a pity we couldn't
Meet where others could watch us,
With room for ourselves and an audience!
I'd love to have them see
Who was the better knight.   1635
But that's that: let's find
Some nearby field, open
And large enough for combat."
So they rode along, and came
To a meadow crowded with girls   1640
And knights and ladies, playing
All sorts of games, enjoying

The pleasures of that lovely spot.
And most enjoyed no simple
Childish sports, but chess,   1645
And backgammon, while others
Played dominoes, and games
Of dice on metal boards.
But some among them strummed
Lutes, and others amused   1650
Themselves like children, dancing
Around in circles, singing
As they went, jumping and tumbling
Down.
      In the far corner
Of the field, an elderly knight   1655
Sat on a sorrel Spanish
Stallion with gilded saddle
And reins. His hair was grizzled
And gray. He sat striking
A pose, his hand on his hip,   1660
And watched, wearing nothing
Over his shirt, in such fine
Weather; his scarlet, fur-trimmed
Cloak lay back on his shoulders.
On a path nearby, awaiting   1665
His orders, were twenty-three knights,
Armed, and on excellent Irish
Horses. But all the games
Were over, the moment the travelers
Arrived. Everyone shouted,   1670
"See! See! It's the knight
Who rode in the cart! No one
Can go on playing, as long

As he's here! Even wanting
To play in his presence would be   1675
Unlucky, but daring to try it
Would surely be cursed." Meanwhile,
The boastful young knight, madly
In love with the girl, confident
He'd finally caught her, approached   1680
The gray-haired elderly knight,
Who happened to be his father.
"My lord," he declared, "I'm wonderfully
Happy, and I want the world
To hear it. God in His goodness   1685
Has given me what I've always desired:
Crowning me king wouldn't have been
Better or made me more grateful
Or granted me more. I've won
Goodness and beauty both!"   1690
"I'm not so sure she's yours."
The old knight said to his son,
Who answered at once: "Not sure?
Is there something wrong with your eyes?
By God, don't doubt me, father;   1695
Just look for yourself. I've got her,
I caught her there in the forest,
She came riding by, and I got her.
God Himself must have brought her,
Made her mine by right."   1700
"I doubt that knight who followed you
Here will let you have her.
I suspect he'll challenge your claim."
While they were talking, the whole
Assembly stood still, no one   1705

Wanting to play or dance,
Filled with loathing for our knight—
Who hurried over to the girl
And stayed at her side. "Release
The young lady, knight," he said.   1710
"You have no right to detain her.
And if you insist, here
And now I'll fight you in her name."
At which the elderly knight
Exclaimed, "I told you, didn't I?   1715
My son, give the girl
Her freedom, let him have her."
Deeply upset, the young
Knight swore he'd never
Surrender what he'd won, declaring,   1720
"Let God deprive me of all
Life's pleasures, if I let her go!
It was I who won her, and I'll
Keep her: she belongs to me!
I'd rather strip my shield   1725
Of every buckle and strap,
And lose all faith in myself,
My arm, my armor, my sword
And my spear, and all I am,
Than give up this girl I love!"   1730
"I won't let you fight," said his father,
"Whatever you say. You think
Better of yourself than you should.
Listen to me, and obey."
But his proud son replied,   1735
"Do you think I'm a child, who needs
To be frightened? Let me tell you:

Nowhere in this world surrounded
By oceans is there a knight
Brave and strong enough   1740
To make me let her go
Without a fight. And I'll beat him."
But his father replied, "So
You believe, my son; clearly,
Your trust in yourself is immense.   1745
No matter: I won't let you
Engage this knight in combat."
The young man answered, "What a coward
I'd be, to take your advice.
And anyone else who listens   1750
To you and refuses to fight me
Can go straight to the devil!
By God: buying at home
Makes bad bargains. I'd better
Leave, since you'd like to cheat me.   1755
I can prove my courage elsewhere.
People who've never seen me
Won't feel obliged to stand
In my way, tormenting and destroying,
As you have. What hurts the most   1760
Is your harsh scolding—as if
You didn't know, and surely
You do, that blocking desire,
A man's or a woman's, can only
Whip the flame higher. If I give up   1765
Anything on your account,
May God deny me joy
Forever. I'm fighting, in spite
Of you." "By Saint Peter and the Pope,"

Said the father, "now I see   1770
Words are wasted on you.
I can't teach you a thing.
Enough talking: let me
Quickly make sure you do
What I tell you, not what you want,   1775
For my will will prevail."
He called to the knights who'd come
With him, ordering them all
To lay hold of this son who refused
To obey his father. And then   1780
He told them, "Before I let him
Fight, I'll tie him up.
I've made you all what you are:
You owe me your faith and your love.
In the name of all I have offered you,   1785
These are my orders. Obey them.
Impelled by his swollen pride,
This son of mine acts
Like a fool, disdaining my wishes."
As one, they promised to lock   1790
His unruly son in their arms,
Completely unable to fight,
And they'd force him to give up the girl,
Whether he liked it or not.
And then they all grasped him,   1795
Some by the arms, some
Round the neck. "Now!" said the father.
"Can you see what a fool you've been?
No matter what you do,
Or what you think, or how   1800
You feel, or how much it hurts,

You can't fight any battles.
If you've got any sense, you'll let
Yourself be guided by me.
Do you know what I think?   1805
To help you feel better, we'll follow
This knight, in daylight and darkness,
If you like, over the fields
And through the forests, riding
Quietly along behind him.   1810
That way we'll see what sort
Of knight he is, and whether
I can agree to let you
Measure your skill against his."
And although it grated on his heart,   1815
The son was obliged to consent,
There being no other choice
But to force himself to be patient,
And follow the knight, and wait.
And all the people in the meadow,   1820
Having seen what happened,
Turned to each other and said,
"Did you see? The knight of the cart
Just won the honor of leading
Away the girl beloved   1825
By our lord's son, and they're following
Him. By God, there must be
Something to him, or they'd never
Let him have her. And now,
A hundred curses on anyone   1830
Who won't go back to our games!
Let's play!" And they all returned
To their games, and their dances and songs.

But our knight rode right off,
Not lingering there in those fields,   1835
And the girl rode along
Behind him, not needing to be led.
And they both rode rapidly.
Father and son followed them
At a distance; by noon, jogging   1840
Across a mown field,
They came to a monastery
Church, in a lovely setting,
With a walled graveyard beside it.
Being neither a peasant   1845
Nor a fool, our knight went into
The church to pray, while the girl
Remained behind, watching
His horse. And having said
His prayers, he was heading back   1850
Outside when he saw an ancient
Monk walking along
And stopped to greet him. And then,
In a gentle voice, he asked
The old man to tell him what   1855
Was behind the walls, for he did not
Know. A cemetery,
The monk replied. "Show me,
Please," said our knight, "in the name
Of God." "Gladly, my lord."   1860
So the monk led him into
The graveyard, where he saw the most beautiful
Tombs to be seen from there
To Dombes or Pampelona,
Each inscribed with the names   1865

Of those who were meant to lie there
When their time came. And our knight
Began to read those inscriptions,
And found the following: "Here
Gawain will lie, and here   1870
Loholt, Arthur's son,
And here Yvain"—and a host
Of other noble knights,
The bravest and best in all
Of France and the rest of the world.   1875
And then he saw a marble
Tomb, and it seemed to him
Lovelier than anything there.
So he called to the ancient monk,
Asking, "For whom are these tombs   1880
Intended?" The old man answered,
"You've seen what's written here.
If you understand these words
You already know what they say
And for whom these tombs are waiting."   1885
"But that huge and lovely one bears
No name. Who will lie there?"
"I'll tell you," said the hermit. "This tomb
Is the grandest ever made
Anywhere here on this earth.   1890
No one has ever seen
Such rich, luxuriant work:
It's lovelier inside than out.
But don't imagine you'll ever
Get to see for yourself.   1895
That will never happen.
Seven strapping men

Would be needed to open this tomb,
If anyone wanted to look,
For it's sealed by a huge stone.   1900
Seven men, all stronger
Than you or me, would surely
Be needed to lift it. Or even
More. It's inscribed with these words:
'He who raises this stone,   *another test*   1905
Using only the strength
Of his own body, will free
From worldly confinement all those—
Peasants, and men of noble
Birth—who lie behind bars   1910
In a prison from which no one returns;
They're locked in that faraway place,
Though those who reside in that distant
Land come and go
As they please.'" The knight took hold   1915
Of the huge stone, which he lifted
As if it were light as a feather,
Though ten men heaving
As hard as they could couldn't do it.
The ancient monk was so   1920
Astonished he almost fell over;
He'd never seen such a miracle,
And never expected to see one
As long as he lived. And he said,
"My lord, you've made me most   1925
Anxious to know your name.
Would you tell me, please?" "Me?
No, by God!" said the knight.
"Ah, I'm sorry," said the monk.

"But if you would, you'd be wonderfully   1930
Gracious and polite, nor
Would the knowledge do you any harm.
Where do you come from—what land?"
"I'm a knight; you can see for yourself;
I was born in the kingdom of Logres.   1935
I hope that tells you enough.
Now tell me, please, as you said
You would, who's meant to lie
In this tomb." "Whoever can free
Those prisoners held without ransom   1940
In that land from which none escape."
The monk having told what he knew,
The knight commended his soul
To God and all His saints,
And then, as quickly as he could,   1945
Returned to the girl, who was waiting.
The white-haired monk went with him,
Escorting him out of the church,
And while the girl remounted,
Ready to resume their journey,   1950
The monk hurriedly told her
All that the knight had done,
And begged her, if she knew his name,
To kindly tell it, but let it
Be known, too, if she did not   1955
Know. But all she dared
Say was this: no knight
In the four corners of the world
Would ever be his equal.
          And then she left him, and galloped   1960
After the knight. In

The meantime, the two who'd been following
Behind them arrived, and the monk,
Alone in front of the church,
Saw them. The elderly knight   1965
Asked, "Sir, tell us:
Have you seen a knight leading
A young woman?" The monk
Replied, "It's easy enough
To tell you whatever I know,   1970
For they've just ridden away.
But before he left, that knight
Entered our church, and all
Alone performed a wondrous
Deed, for he lifted—without   1975
Struggling, without hurting
Himself—a huge stone
From a marble tomb. He means
To rescue the queen, and he will,
And all the other prisoners.   1980
You know what's written on that stone,
My lords, you've often read
The inscription. No knight his equal
Has ever been born to human
Flesh or sat in a saddle."   1985
The old knight spoke to the young one,
"What do you think, my son?
What kind of knight performs
Such feats? And who was wrong,
Eh—you or me?   1990
Not for all the wealth
In Amiens would I have you
Fight him! You'd better think,

And think long and hard, if you shouldn't
Turn around and go home,   1995
For you'd be an absolute fool
To go on following behind him."
And the young knight replied, "I agree.
Pursuing him would be worthless.
As long as you're willing, let's leave."   2000
It made a great deal of sense.
And all this time the girl
Rode along beside
Our knight, trying to talk him
Into telling his name,   2005
Asking him over and over,
Never accepting no
For an answer. And finally he said,
"Haven't I told you I come
From King Arthur's court? In the name   2010
Of God Almighty, I swear
I'll never tell you my name!"
So she asked permission to leave,
Promising to come back, and the knight
Was delighted to let her go.   2015
        So the girl rode away,
And the knight, knowing he was late,
Galloped on alone.
In the late afternoon, as night-song
Was sung, he was riding hard   2020
And saw a knight returning
From the woods, where he'd spent the day
Hunting. He rode on his great
Stallion, his helmet laced on,
And the deer that God had granted him   2025

[margin note:] why, doesn't he say?

Hung across his horse,
And he came quickly, hurrying
To greet the knight of the cart
And ask him to lodge at his home.
"Sir," he said, "it's late,   2030
And time to be off the road;
It makes sense to look for lodging.
I have a house nearby,
To which I'd be glad to take you.
There's nowhere you'd be a more welcome   2035
Guest; I'll do all I can.
Please make me happy and accept."
"I'd be pleased to come," said our knight.
The host immediately sent
His son ahead, to make   2040
Sleeping arrangements and ensure
That supper was served on time.
The young man galloped off,
Delighted to do exactly
As his father ordered, glad   2045
To have such a guest and more
Than willing to serve him. The two
Knights, having no need
To hurry, ambled along
The road, till they reached the house.   2050
The host had married an amiable,
Well-bred woman; they'd had
Five beloved sons,
Two who were knights, three
Who were squires, plus a pair of lovely   2055
Young girls. Not born in that land,
But in the kingdom of Logres,

They were treated as foreign prisoners,
Having been held in confinement
For a very long time. The father   2060
Of the family ushered his guest
Into their courtyard, and his wife
Came hurrying out to greet them,
Followed by his sons and daughters,
All offering to serve and assist.   2065
Our knight greeted them all
And dismounted. But neither the girls
Nor their five brothers waited
On his host, well aware
What their father wanted done.   2070
They showered the guest with honors.
And when they'd taken his arms
And armor, one of his host's
Daughters took off her cloak
And wrapped it around his shoulders.   2075
I hardly need to tell you
How well he dined, that night.
And once their dinner was done,
They talked freely, discussing
All manner of things. The host   2080
Began by asking their guest
Who he was and where
He came from, but never asking
His name. The knight of the cart
Answered at once: "I come   2085
From the kingdom of Logres; I've never
Been in this land before."
Hearing this, his host,
And his host's wife and children,

Were deeply affected, all   2090
Uttering sighs and groans.
And then they told him, "Oh good
Sweet sir, how sad that you've come,
What a terrible shame! For now
You'll become, as we all are,   2095
Slaves and servants in exile."
"In exile from where?" he asked.
"My lord, from Logres, like you.
This prison holds many
Brave and noble souls   2100
From our land. May this savage custom
Be cursed, and those who keep it!
For no stranger who comes here
Is ever allowed to leave,
Tied forever to this land. serfs   2105
No one's denied entrance,
But once they're here, they must stay.
Your fate, too, is determined:
I doubt you'll ever leave."
"Oh yes, I will, if I can."   2110
The host shook his head:
"Really? You think you can go
As you came?" "Indeed, with God's
Blessing. I'll certainly try."
"Then, surely, none of the others   2115
Will be afraid to follow
After, for if one can safely
Leave, and escape this prison,
Nothing can hold the rest,
And no one will try to stop them."   2120
And then the host remembered

A rumor sweeping the land,
That a great and powerful knight
Had stormed across their border,
Come to rescue the queen   2125
Held captive by Méléagant.
The king's son: "It's him,"
He thought. "I must say so."
"My lord," he said, "hide
Nothing from me, and in   2130
Return you'll have the best
Advice I'm able to give.
I stand to gain, if you
Can do what you mean to. So tell me
The truth, on your own account   2135
As well as mine. I already
Know you've come to this country
In search of the queen—here
Among this infidel race,
Worse than the Moslem hordes."   2140
The knight of the cart answered,
"I've no other reason for coming.
I've no idea where they're holding
My lady, but all I want
Is to help her, and I need advice.   2145
Counsel me, please, if you can."
His host answered, "My lord,
You've begun a dangerous business.
The road you're on is leading you
Straight to the Sword Bridge.   2150
Now is when you need
Advice. If you'll listen to me,
You'll approach the Sword Bridge

By a very much safer route:
I'll show you the way." But our knight,   2155
Who had no interest in a shorter
Road, replied, "Is your route
Just as direct as mine?"
"No," was the answer. "It's longer,
Because it's so much safer."   2160
"Then it's not the road I want,"
Said the knight. "Now tell me, if you know,
Just what I'm likely to meet."
"My lord, your road's not useful.
If you go that way, tomorrow   2165
You'll come to a corridor you might
Be sorry to travel; it's called
THE STONY PATH. Would you like me
To tell you exactly why
It's so exceedingly dangerous?   2170
It's precisely the width of a horse:
Two men side by side
Can't get through, and it's well
Watched and fiercely guarded.
They'll come running to stop you   2175
The moment you appear. Expect
A shower of sword blows and spear thrusts,
And plan to give as many
Back, before you cross over."
As soon as he'd finished speaking,   2180
A knight stepped forward, one
Of the host's sons, who said,
"My lord, with your permission
I'd like to go with him, if you please."
And one of his other sons,   2185

A squire, said, "I'd like
To go, too." The father gladly
Gave his consent to them both.
Pleased not to be
Alone, our knight thanked them;   2190
Their company would be very welcome.
   The conversation over,
Our knight lay down to sleep,
For he badly needed rest.
But as soon as the sun's light   2195
Could be seen, he rose, and those
Who'd agreed to travel with him
Immediately left their beds.
They put on their armor and took
Their weapons, made their farewells,   2200
And left. The squire led them,
And they rode on together,
Till early that morning they reached
The Stony Path. A small
Fort barred the way,   2205
With a sentinel standing inside.
They drew near, and as
They approached he saw them, and began
To cry, as loud as he could,
"Enemy alert! Enemy   2210
Alert!" And then a mounted
Knight in dazzling new
Armor rode out from the fort,
And soldiers with sharp axes
Appeared from every side.   2215
And as the knight of the cart
Came closer, the knight-defender

Hurled insulting words:
"Fellow," he called, "you're a stubborn
Fool, coming so far   2220
Across this land. Once
He's ridden in a cart, no knight
Should dare show his face
Here. God won't let you
Rejoice at making this trip!"   2225
Then he and our knight spurred
Their horses straight ahead.
The defender thrust so hard   *bad moment*
With his lance that it broke in two,
And the pieces fell to the ground.   2230
But our knight's blow, just
Above the edge of the shield,
Struck the defender's throat
And threw him down on the rocks.
His soldiers ran forward, their axes   2235
Raised, but careful that none
Of their blows hurt our knight
Or his horse. He saw at once
Their attack was all for show
And they meant him no harm, and without   2240
So much as drawing his sword
Rode quickly on, and his two
Companions followed after.
And the younger said to the older
There'd never been such a knight;   2245
No one could possibly match him.
"What an incredible feat,
Breaking through that defense!"
"By God, hurry back,

Brother," said the older, "and find   2250
Our father, and tell him the whole
Story." He was already
A knight. But the young squire
Swore both up and down
He'd never go back or leave   2255
The knight of the cart until
He'd been made a knight at his hands.
If his brother wanted to tell
The story, let him go back
Himself! And off they rode,   2260
The three together, till just about
Noon, when they met with a man.
He asked them who they were,
And they answered, "We're knights, minding
Our business and doing what we should."   2265
And the man said to our knight,
"My lord, I offer food
And shelter to you and your friends."
He addressed our knight, who was clearly
The lord and master of the three.   2270
"I can't imagine stopping
At this hour," said our knight. "Only
Lazy cowards lie
Around at their ease, when there's work
Like this to be done. The task   2275
I've undertaken is so
Important I can't stop now!"
Then the man replied, "Ah,
We're nowhere near where I live:
It's still a good long ride.   2280
The hour will be late, when you get there,

Let me assure you, and the time
Will be right for seeking shelter."
"Agreed," said our knight. "I'll come."
They rode on down the road,   2285
The man leading the way,
The knight of the cart and the others
Behind him. They'd been riding a while
When a squire came dashing toward them,
Down the same road, mounted   2290
On a nag as fat and round
As an apple. And he said to the man,
"My lord, my lord, come quick!
The people of Logres have taken up
Arms and invaded our land,   2295
The battle's already under
Way, men are screaming
And fighting all over the place.
And they're saying a knight who's fought
All over the world has crossed   2300
Into this country, and no one's
Strong enough to block
His way, he goes wherever
He wants, no matter who tries
To stop him. And they say he'll free   2305
All the prisoners, and grind
The others into the ground.
So hurry, please. Hurry!"
The man whipped up his horse.
But the others were wonderfully happy,   2310
For they too had heard
The squire, and wanted to help
Their people. "My lord," said the host's

Sons, "you've heard this fellow.
We ought to hurry, too,   2315
And help our people fight."
Their guide had galloped ahead,
Not waiting, riding as fast
As he could toward a fortress built
Into the rise of a hill,   2320
And heading directly for the gate.
They galloped after him. The fort
Was surrounded by a high wall
And encircled by a moat. But the very
Moment they dashed in   2325
Behind him, a great gate
Came crashing down on their heels,
Blocking the way back.
"Go on, go on!" they shouted.
"We can't stop here!"   2330
Hurrying after their guide
They saw him ride unharmed,
Unhindered, clear through
The exit door, but as soon
As he'd gotten past it, another   2335
Gate was dropped behind him.
And then they were deeply concerned,
Seeing themselves shut in
And thinking there was magic at work.
But the knight of the cart, of whom   2340
I've more to tell you, wore
A ring on his finger, and its stone
Possessed the power to break
Any enchantment its owner
Encountered. He held the stone   2345

High, and stared in its depths,
And said, "Oh Lady, Lady,
If God wishes to help me
Now is my time of need."
    The Lady of the Lake was a fairy   2350
Who'd tended him as a child;
She'd given him this ring.
No matter where he might be,
He knew she'd come to his aid
If ever magic threatened.   2355
But after calling her name,
And studying the stone, he saw
Quite clearly this was not magic:
They were simply well and truly
Trapped, shut in a prison.   2360
They saw, to one side, a small
Door, shut and barred
Against them, and drawing their swords
As one, they cut and slashed
So fiercely that the bar fell away.   2365
They ran out of the tower
And saw the battle had begun,
Fierce and savage, involving
At least a thousand knights
On both sides, not counting   2370
A huge crowd of peasants.
And as they made their way down
To the field, the host's son
Spoke these prudent, sensible
Words, "My lord, I think   2375
We'd be wise, before we enter
The combat, to be sure we know

Where the men on our side are fighting.
I'm not yet sure myself,
But I'll go and see, if you like."   2380
"Go," said our knight, "and quickly,
And come back as fast as you can."
He hurried off, then hurried
Back. "How lucky we are!
There's not a doubt in my mind: 2385
These men right here are ours."
The knight of the cart ran
Directly into battle,
And found a knight hurrying
To meet him. He struck one blow   2390
And laid him dead on the ground.
The young squire climbed down
And took the dead knight's horse,
And the handsome armor he'd worn,
And made himself ready to fight.   2395
Without wasting a word
He mounted and took up the shield
And the heavy, painted spear,
Then hung the brightly glittering,
Razor-sharp sword on his belt.   2400
And into battle he went,
Following both his brother
And his lord, who'd been fighting well,
All this time, smashing
And shattering shields and helmets,   2405
Cracking and splitting mail shirts.
Neither wood nor iron could keep
Their lord from wounding his enemies,
Sweeping them, dead, down

From their saddles. All by himself   2410
He might have won the battle,
And the two who fought beside him
Nicely reinforced
His efforts. The men of Logres
Were amazed, not knowing who   2415
He was, and many turned
To the host's son, hunting
His name. "Gentlemen," he said,
"He's come to lead us out
Of exile and end the misery   2420
We've suffered so long. Show him
All the honor you can:
For our sake, he's met with
Terrible dangers, and will meet
With many more. He's accomplished   2425
Much. But there's still much
To be done." They were overjoyed,
As the news spread through their ranks;
All had heard he would come,
All had longed to see him.   2430
Their excitement grew and grew
Until it gave them such strength
That they killed their enemies like flies,
And would have killed many more—
Though mostly, it seems to me,   2435
The work was done by one
Knight in particular. But night
Was starting to fall, and it saved
The opposing army from disaster,
Covering the world in darkness   2440
And forcing the fighting to stop.

The battle interrupted,
The former prisoners crowded
Around the knight, almost
Quarreling, fighting for his reins,   2445
And all of them crying at once:
"Welcome, welcome, my lord!"
And each of them said, "My lord,
Come stay with me; my lord,
In the name of God, please,   2450
Don't stay with anyone else."
They were all saying the same
Thing, for young and old
Were hungry to have him as their guest:
"You'd be better off staying   2455
With me than with anyone else."
They circled around him, each
Trying to outdo the other,
Pushing and shoving and very
Nearly coming to blows.   2460
And finally the knight told them
It was all foolish noise:
"Stop this stupid bickering,"
He said. "It's a waste of time.
We mustn't argue among   2465
Ourselves, but help each other.
You've got no business quarreling
Like this, about where I sleep:
You ought to be thinking, instead,
How to put me up   2470
For the night somewhere close
To the road I need to take."
And still they argued on:

"Mine is the best!—No, mine!"
"I'm still not hearing," said the knight,   2475
"What I'd like to hear: these noises
You're making tell me the smartest
Man among you is a fool.
You ought to be urging me on,
But all you're doing is setting up   2480
Detours. To do things as they should have
Been done, you'd each and all
Offer as much honor
And help as a man could want,
And then, by all the saints   2485
In Rome, I'd be as grateful
To everyone here for your actions
As in fact I am for your fine
Intentions. May God give me health
And joy, but I find myself   2490
Already as grateful to you all
As if you'd done me wonderful
Favors—and the will can stand for
The act!" And so he calmed them,
And they led him off to a rich knight's   2495
Home, right on the road
He was traveling, and each of them honored
And served him, at great expense,
And until they went to their beds
A great good time was had   2500
By all, for everyone loved him.
In the morning, when he had to leave,
Everyone wanted to ride
With him, anxious to help,
But he had no interest in anyone   2505

Joining his journey except
The two who'd come with him
When he first arrived: he'd take
These two, and no one else.
They rode quietly, that day,   2510
From morning to night, without
Meeting a single adventure.
Then, galloping hard, late
In the day, they emerged from a wood
And as they broke from the trees   2515
Saw a knight's house,
And his gracious-seeming lady
Seated in front of the door.
The moment she saw them coming
She rose to greet them, her face   2520
Fairly glowing with pleasure:
"Welcome," she said warmly.
"I'd like you to stay at my home;
Please be my guests—dismount."
"Your wish is our command,   2525
Lady. We will dismount
And spend the night here."
Once they were down, she arranged
For their horses to be led away,
For hers was a noble house.   2530
She called her sons and daughters,
Who came at once—courteous,
Amiable youngsters, her sons
Handsome, her daughters lovely—
And told them to remove the saddles   2535
And take good care of the beasts.
They obeyed her without a murmur,

Cheerfully doing her will.
And her daughters helped the travelers
Out of their armor, and when this   2540
Was done they draped over
Their shoulders three short cloaks.
And then they were shown straight
To their rooms, which were very beautiful.
Although the lord of the house   2545
Was not there—he had gone hunting
In the woods, with two of his sons—
He was expected any minute,
And the well-trained servants were waiting
In front of the door. He arrived,   2550
And the dead deer were quickly
Untied and carried in,
And the servants told him the news:
"You don't know it yet, my lord,
But you've three knights as your guests."   2555
"God be praised!" he replied.
The knight and his two sons
Were delighted to meet their guests,
And the servants were hardly asleep:
Each and all were ready   2560
To do what they needed to do,
Some hurrying to prepare
Food, and others fetching
Candles, which they quickly lit,
While others brought in basins,   2565
So the guests could wash their hands—
And how they poured out water!
And when they had washed, dinner
Was served. Nothing could be seen

On that table to offend anyone!   2570
And then, as the first course came,
They were treated to the presence, outside
The door, of a knight as swollen
With pride as an arrogant bull.
He was armored from head to foot   2575
And mounted on a great stallion;
One leg was in the stirrups,
The other was thrown, with an air
Of supreme indifference, over
His horse's neck, on its mane.   2580
No one had seen him come
Until, all of a sudden,
There he was. "Who's
The one," he asked, "tell me,
So proud, and also so stupid,   2585
Blessed with so brainless a skull,
That he's ridden all this way
Intending to cross the Sword
Bridge? He's wasted his time
And his effort, he's come here for nothing."   2590
The knight of the cart calmly
Answered, not in the least
Impressed: "I'm the one."
"You? What put the idea
In your head? What you should have done,   2595
Before you started this business,
Was think how it all might end
For someone who'd ridden in a cart—
Or had you forgotten all that?
Did you remember? Are you   2600
Truly as shameless as you seem?

But no one could be so foolish
As to take on a task this grand,
Knowing himself stained
With such a blemish." Our knight   2605
Listened to this talk, but didn't
Bother to respond. But everyone
Else around his host's
Table was stunned, as well
They might have been: "Oh Lord!   2610
What a horrible thing," they said
To one another. "What
A revolting invention! Curse
The hour when the cart was conceived!
How vile, how disgusting. Oh Lord: 2615
What could he be accused of?
Why was he put in a cart?
What crime could he have committed?
He'll never be allowed to forget it.
Except for this, only   2620
This, you could search the whole
Wide world and never find
A knight to match him, no matter
Who he was or what
He'd done. Put them all   2625
In one place, and none would be
As handsome, as noble. None."
And everyone there agreed.
But the arrogant knight outside
The door spoke again,   2630
Saying, "Listen, you,
Before you attempt that bridge:
If you like, I'll show you an easy

Way, and a safe one, to get
Across. I'll ferry you over   2635
On a boat, and do it quickly.
But the price I'll ask, once
I've got you there, will be
Your head, if I feel like having it—
Or not. The choice will be mine."   2640
But our knight answered he wasn't
Anxious to injure himself:
He wouldn't risk his neck
Like that, no matter the cost.
The arrogant knight continued: 2645
"If you're not willing to try it,
Since either way you'll be shamed
Or sorrowful, you'll have to step
Outside so we can fight."
And our knight answered, dryly,   2650
"If I had a choice, I think
I'd just as soon not bother,
But I'd much prefer fighting
To dealing with things still worse."
And then, before he rose   2655
From the table, he asked those
Who served him to have his horse
Saddled as soon as possible,
And also to bring his armor
And weapons, ready for use.   2660
They quickly did as he asked,
Some swiftly helping
With his armor, others with his horse—
And let me tell you, by God,
That astride his steed, armor   2665

Gleaming, his shield hung
Across his breast, his lance
In his hand, prepared for combat—
No one would have been wrong,
Counting him one of the fairest   2670
And best! Who could have known
His horse was borrowed? and the shield
He carried? and the helmet laced
Around his head? Everything
Perfectly suited his looks;   2675
His manners, his bearing, balanced them
So well that no one could ever
Have imagined they were only on loan.
No: seeing his splendor
You'd have sworn it had all been his   2680
From birth. Believe me, it's the truth.
      Outside the gate was a field
With room enough, as the rules
Require, for the battle to be fought.
Turning, they looked at each other   2685
And immediately spurred their horses
To a furious, headlong charge,
Thrusting their spears so fiercely
That they bent like bows and quickly
Splintered to pieces. Then they drew   2690
Their swords and smashed them against
Shields and helmets and mail shirts,
Slicing away wood and cracking
Iron, till both were wounded,
And their angry blows came clanking   2695
Down like coins being paid
For a debt. But many of the blows

Fell on the horses' rumps,
And stallions and men alike
Were bathed in blood, for the ravenous   2700
Swords brought death to the beasts.   *oh no*
So tumbling out of the saddle
They fought each other on foot,
Driven by mortal hatred;
Such savage assaults are rare,   2705
Such brutal sword blows and determined,
Murderous attack. They hammered
At one another faster
Than gamblers rattling dice,
Both of them desperate to win,   2710
Never pausing for breath,
But playing a far more deadly
Game, in which chance had no role
But only mortal battle-
Strokes. People poured out   2715
To watch, men and women,
Girls and boys, till the house
Was empty of family and guests
And everyone stood at the edge
Of the broad meadow, staring   2720
As the combat swung this way and that.
Seeing his host among them,
The knight of the cart cursed
Himself for his failure, and then,
Seeing that literally everyone   2725
Was watching, he began to shake
With anger, for as far as he
Was concerned, he should have finished
This battle long ago.

Exploding out at his enemy   2730
Like a wild storm, he struck
So close to the arrogant knight's
Head that he had to step back,
And our knight pursued him, pressed him,
Forcing him around and around   2735
The field until the breath
Left his body and he could not
Fight. Our knight could not
Forget how meanly the man
Had thrown in his face the little   2740
Trip in the cart. He quickly
Sliced away straps
And laces, opening the armor
That protected the neck, and then
Was able to knock the helmet   2745
Off his head; it rolled
On the ground, and our knight stabbed
And struck till the other, like a swallow
Helpless in front of a hawk,
So beaten down by his claws   2750
And wings, utterly
Defeated, drained, had no choice
But to beg for his life. Miserable
And shamed, there was nothing else
He could do. And hearing this request   2755
For mercy, the knight of the cart
Stood very still, saying,
"You wish me to grant you mercy?"
"That shows how wise you are,"
Said the beaten man. "Any fool   2760
Knows that. I've never wanted

A thing as much as I long for
Mercy!" "But in order to get it
You'll have to ride in a cart.
Don't bother telling me all   2765
The clever things you can think of:
Because your stupid mouth
Threw such vile words
At me, you'll ride in a cart."
And the arrogant knight answered,   2770
"May God keep it away!"
"Really? If He does, you die."
"That's up to you, my lord.
In the name of God, I beg you
For mercy, asking only   2775
That I not be put in a cart.
I'm ready to receive any
Pain or punishment but that:
I'd much prefer to be dead
Than suffer such misery. Apart   2780
From that, I accept whatever
Price you may choose to ask
As payment for your mercy and grace."
    While they bargained for the man's
Life, a girl came riding   2785
Across the field, mounted
On a tawny mule; she wore
No hat, and her hair waved
In the wind. She was using her whip
So freely and well that although   2790
No mule can truly gallop,
This one was ambling at remarkable
Speed. She approached our knight

And said, "May God grant you,
Knight, perfect peace   2795
And happiness, whatever you want."
He heard her with pleasure, and answered,
"May God bless you, girl,
And bring you health and joy."
And then she told him what she wanted: 2800
"Knight, I've come a long
Way, and in great need,
To ask you to grant me a wish,
In return for which I promise
To give you the greatest   2805
Reward I know of—and one
Day, I believe, you're going
To need my help." The knight
Replied, "Tell me your wish,
And if it's in my power   2810
I'll grant it at once, provided
It's not too painful or hard."
And she said, "All I want
Is that knight's head, the one
You've just defeated. Truly,   2815
You'll never find a more evil
Man. It won't be sinful
To kill him, but a pious good deed:
Believe me, he's the worst man
Alive or who ever lived."   2820
When the beaten man heard
That she wanted him killed, he said,
"Don't believe her: she hates me.
Again, in the name of God
Who is Father and Son I beg you,   2825

For Him who chose as His mother
His own daughter and servant,
To show me mercy." "Ha!"
Said the girl. "I beg you, knight:
Don't believe this traitor.   2830
May God grant you all
The honor and happiness you want,
And bless you with the power to accomplish
The task you've undertaken!"
The knight was so caught betwixt   2835
And between that he stopped, suspended
In thought, uncertain whether
To cut off the head she wanted
Or grant mercy to the beaten
Man begging for his life.   2840
He wished he could give each of them
Exactly what they'd asked for:
Our knight was kind and generous,
So Pity and Generosity
Pulled him in both directions.   2845
If he gave her the knight's head
Pity would suffer and die,
And if he refused her he'd kill off
Generosity.
Each emotion held him,   2850
Pressed him, pulled him, each one
Pierced his heart, and he suffered.
The girl was crying, "Cut off
His head and let me have it!"
While the knight demanded mercy   2855
And release, in pity's name.
And since he'd begged for his life

Shouldn't it be restored?
Indeed! Once the battle
Was won, and his enemy beaten,   2860
He'd never refused mercy
To anyone, no matter who—
Never. Once it was asked for
It was granted. His mercy was always
Available, though no one could ask   2865
For more. Whoever begged
For his life would have it: that
Had always been his custom.
But should she have the knight's
Head? Yes—if he   2870
Could give it. "Knight," he said,
"You need to fight me again,
And if you wish to defend
Your head, I'll grant you that favor,
Allow you to take back your helmet   2875
And arm yourself once more,
At whatever pace you choose
And as best you can. But let it
Be clear: if I vanquish you
Again, you're going to die."   2880
"Exactly what I want," said the other.
"It's the only mercy I ask for."
"But I'll grant you more," said our knight.
"I'll fight this battle standing
Right where I am, not moving   2885
In any direction." The beaten
Knight made ready, and they went
To work with a will, but this time
Victory came neither as slow

Nor as hard: our knight defeated   2890
The other one swiftly and well.
And the girl quickly called out,
"Don't spare him again, no matter
What he tells you! He'd never
Have shown you mercy, if he'd   2895
Had the chance. Believe me, I know him.
Let him talk and he'll spin
A web of words around you.
This is the most disloyal
And treacherous head in the kingdom: 2900
Cut it off, good knight, and give it
To me. You ought to, believe me,
For there'll come a time, I know it,
When I'll be able to pay you
Back. But listen to him   2905
And you're likely to lose everything."
And the beaten knight, seeing
Death so close, began
To cry and wail, but it did him
No good, and neither did his words.   2910
Our knight grasped him by the helmet
So fiercely that the straps and laces
Broke, and all the supporting
Gear fell away, and his head
Was bare. He cried even louder: 2915
"Oh God, mercy, mercy!"
"May God save my soul," said our knight,
"You've had all the mercy
I can give you. I have no more."
"Ah, what a ghastly sin   2920
You're committing," he wailed, "murdering

Me on my enemy's word!"
And the girl, longing for his head,
Urged our knight to quickly
Cut it off and stop   2925
Listening to his lying words.
One swing of the sword, the head
Was off, and it and the body
Fell to the ground. And the girl
Was happy. Our knight picked up   2930
The head and put it in her hands,
And she smiled with satisfaction
And said, "May your heart have the joy
It most wants in this world,
As I do now, having   2935
This head I hate so much.
Seeing him live so long
Was the only affliction I knew.
You've done me a great service;
You may be sure I'll repay you.   2940
Expect your reward to come
When it's most needed—believe me.
And now I will leave you. Go
With God. May He guard you from danger."
He, too, commended her   2945
To God, and then she left.
But among the men of that country
Who had seen the battle, an immense
Joy grew and swelled.
Happy and laughing, they helped   2950
Our knight remove his armor,
Then showered him with honors.
Once again they washed

His hands and offered him food,
And the table rang with their great,   2955
Their deep and unusual, pleasure.
They dined slowly, and well,
And finally our knight's host,
Seated beside him, declared,
"My lord, it's been a long time   2960
Since we came here from Logres. We were born
In that land, so we wish enormous
Rewards and endless honor
And joy to be yours, and we long
To share with you, and with many   2965
Others, all the success
And glory you may find here,
As you finish what you've so well begun."
And he answered, "May God hear you!"
      When the host ended his speech,   2970
And the sound of his words had faded,
One of his sons rose
And said, "My lord, we place
Ourselves, as we must, at your service,
Offering you deeds as well   2975
As words. If you wish to accept
Our help, there's no need to wait
Until you're obliged to ask.
Don't worry, my lord, if you think
Your horse is dead: we have   2980
A host of fine horses, and they're yours.
Take the best we have,
In exchange for the one you've lost;
You'll need a good one." And our knight
Answered, "Thank you. I accept   2985

Most gladly." And then their beds
Were made, and they went to sleep.
They rose early in the morning,
And hurried, leaving as soon
As they could. But our knight was careful   2990
To say farewell to his host
And his host's lady, and to all
The others. And there's something else
I need to tell you, for I wish
To omit nothing. Our knight   2995
Refused to mount the horse
Saddled and waiting for his use,
But insisted that one of the two
Knights who'd ridden with him
Be given the gift instead.   3000
He took the other man's horse
For himself, and was pleased to have done it.
And when they were all mounted,
The three of them rode away
With their host's blessing—he   3005
Who had served and honored them all
As well as he possibly could.
Following the most direct
Route, just as the light
Was fading, about nine   3010
That night, they saw the Sword Bridge.
They stopped and dismounted at the foot
Of the terrifying structure, looking
Down at the treacherous water,
Black and boiling, swift   3015
And harsh, as horribly evil
As if it flowed from the devil

Himself, deep and dangerous
Like nothing else in this world:
Whoever fell in would sink   3020
Like a rock in the salty sea.
And the bridge that spanned it was just
As different from other bridges;
Believe me, nothing like it
Had ever existed, or ever   3025
Would, neither as huge
Or as wickedly built—a single
Gleaming sword-blade crossing
That ice-cold water, stiff
And strong, as wide as a pair   3030
Of spears, and attached at either
End to massive tree-trunk
Stumps. No one would worry
About it bending or breaking:
It would clearly stand, no matter   3035
What weight it was asked to bear.
But those who'd come with our knight
Were most concerned at seeing,
Or thinking they saw, a pair
Of lions, or perhaps they were leopards,   3040
Chained to a boulder on the far
Side of the bridge. The water,
The bridge, and the two great beasts
Gave them such a shock
That from head to foot they trembled   3045
With fear: "My lord, allow us
To advise you, seeing what we see,
For advice is what you need.
This bridge is wickedly built,

Evilly put together.   3050
Change your mind now—
Or else you'll lose the chance.
A man must think both long
And hard before he acts.
Suppose you get across—   3055
But it isn't going to happen:
No one can hold back the wind
And stop it from blowing, or forbid
Birds to open their beaks
And sing, and keep them silent,   3060
Or climb into a mother's
Womb and be born again:
All these things are just as
Impossible as draining the sea.
How can you expect   3065
Those furious lions, chained up
Over there, not
To kill you, and drink the blood
From your veins, and swallow your flesh,
And finish by gnawing your bones?   3070
My nerves are strong, but I
Can barely allow my eyes
To see them. If you're not careful,
They'll surely kill you, I know it,
They'll rip you right apart   3075
And tear off your arms and legs.
Expect no mercy: they have none.
So take pity on yourself—
Stay here with us! Don't
Commit so grave a sin   3080
Against yourself, aware

Of mortal risk, yet seeking it
Out." He replied, laughing,
"Gentlemen, I'm deeply grateful
That you care so much for my welfare: 3085
You're good and generous friends.
I know quite well you wish me
To come to no harm. But my faith
In God, my trust in Him,
Compels me to believe He'll protect me.   3090
Neither bridge nor water
Nor this harsh world can worry
Me. I intend to cross,
Whatever the risk. I'd rather
Die than turn and go back!"   3095
There was nothing more to be said,
But pity and sorrow wrung them
Both with bitter tears.
And our knight made ready, as best
He could, to cross the gulf,   3100
Preparing, in the strangest way,
By removing the armor from his hands
And feet, as if making sure
He could not arrive uninjured!
Then he held tight to the sword-blade   3105
Bridge, as sharp as a razor,
Hands and feet both bare—
For he'd left himself no covering,
Neither shoes nor stockings—
Not fearing sharp edges slicing   3110
Away at his flesh, much
Preferring bloody wounds
To falling into that icy

Water from which he would never
Emerge. Accepting the immense   3115
Pain and suffering, he crossed,
Hands and knees and feet
Bleeding. But Love, who had led him
There, helped him as he went,
And turned his pain to pleasure.   3120
When he came to the other side
None of his wounds were hurting.
And then he recalled the pair
Of lions he'd seen, or thought
He'd seen, before he crossed,   3125
But looking here and there
All he could see was a lizard,
And nothing there that could harm him.
Raising his hand to his face
He stared at his ring, and knew   3130
At once the pair of lions
Were imagined, and nowhere in sight,
But conjured out of magic.
There was nothing living to be seen.
And those on the other shore,   3135
Watching him make his way
Across, were overjoyed;
They had not seen his wounds.
But he was sure he'd been blessed,
For it could have been far worse.   3140
Using his shirt, he was drying
The blood running from his wounds
When he noticed, there in front of him,
The tallest, strongest tower
He'd ever seen on this earth: 3145

No one could build a better one!
And leaning out a window
He saw King Bademagu,
A quick-witted man, and wise
In all the ways of honor   3150
And goodness, forever concerned
With keeping the laws of knighthood,
Though his son, standing just
Beside him, was exactly the opposite,
Working to smash and break them   3155
For the sheer joy of deviltry.
Méléagant was never
Tired of base behavior
Of every kind, of treason
And crimes of bad faith. From his post   3160
At the high window, he had watched
The Sword Bridge crossing, with all
Its pain and suffering, and his anger
And outrage brought blood to his face:
He knew he was going to be challenged   3165
For the queen. But he was a prince
Who never felt fear of any
Man, no matter how bold
Or famous. He might have been
The best of knights, had his soul   3170
Been pure, but his heart was cold
As a stone, devoid of pity.
What thrilled the noble father
Pained the son: the king
Knew without a doubt   3175
That the knight who'd crossed the bridge
Was as worthy as anyone ever

Born, for no one stained
With sin would have dared that journey:
Evil deeds shame men   3180
More than good ones help them.
Courage and virtue are lesser
Powers than evil and sloth:
Consider how easy it is
To sin, and how hard to do good.   3185
          I've a lot to say on these subjects,
Which would take me too much time—
And besides, I've other matters
On my mind—so back to my story.
Listen as the king instructs   3190
His son, speaking these words:
"My son, we came to this window,
Just now, by the purest chance,
And stood here, looking out.
And we've been richly repaid,   3195
Allowed to behold the greatest
Feat of courage ever
Attempted, or even imagined.
Tell me: how could you not
Admire such a splendid deed?   3200
Go make your peace with that knight,
And give him back the queen!
You've nothing to win from a quarrel—
Indeed, you've a lot to lose.
Act like a wise and courteous   3205
Man: bring him the queen
Even before he sees you.
Do him the honor, here
In your own land, of handing

Over what he seeks before   3210
He can ask. You cannot doubt
It's Guinevere he's come for.
Don't let yourself be seen
As arrogant, stubborn, or a fool.
And if such a man has come   3215
Alone, join him, be his friend,
Noble hearts must seek
Each other: honor him, praise him,
Don't hold yourself back. Conferring
Honor makes you honorable: 3220
Believe me, you'll honor yourself
In serving and honoring him,
For this, my son, is surely
The greatest knight alive."
"God confound me," was the answer,   3225
"If there isn't one as good—
Or better!" And the father was wrong,
Forgetting his son, who valued
Himself no less. "Perhaps,"
Said the son, "I ought to drop   3230
To my knees and offer my kingdom?
God knows, I'd rather give him
Homage than hand him the queen!
I'll never let him have her.
Anyone who tries to take her   3235
Will have to deal with me:
I'll fight him tooth and nail."
The king continued to press him:
"My son, courtesy requires
Giving up this stubbornness.   3240
Settle this matter in peace.

Don't you see that this knight
Would be shamed, if he didn't defeat you
In battle, and win back the queen?
For him, indeed, victory   3245
In battle would bring more honor
Than taking a gift from your hands.
I doubt he'll want a peaceful
Resolution; he'll try
To settle this by force.   3250
So not permitting him
To fight for what he wants
Would be wise. Your folly disturbs me,
But if you refuse to listen
I can't be much concerned   3255
With your fate, which might be unpleasant:
This knight has nothing to fear
From anyone but you. On behalf
Of my men, and myself, I offer
Him safe conduct and a truce.   3260
In all my life I've never
Broken faith, nor will I now,
Neither for you nor toward
A stranger here in my land.
I won't deceive you, my son: 3265
I hereby vow that this knight
Must have whatever he needs
And lacks, whether weapons or horses.
He's certainly proved his courage,
Coming here as he has,   3270
And his safety will be assured
By every man in this land
Except, alas, by you.

Understand me: if he
Succeeds against you, he need   3275
Not fear anyone else."
"I've listened to every word
You said," was the answer, "and you spoke
A lot of them. I've held my peace.
And still, in the end, you've said   3280
Nothing. I'm no hermit,
No saint all flowing with compassion;
I've no interest in earning
Honor by giving up
My beloved. He won't get her   3285
As fast and easy as that!
Nothing will happen the way
You or he expect.
Help him against me, if you like,
But you and I needn't quarrel.   3290
Offer a truce, you
And your men. What's that to me?
It won't make me afraid!
I'm just as pleased, by God,
That I'll be his only concern.   3295
I won't ask you to help me
Or do a thing that might make you
Guilty of treachery or bad faith.
Go ahead and be good,
And I'll be as cruel as I like."   3300
"What? You'll refuse my advice?"
"Completely." "Then I've nothing to say.
Do as you will. I'll leave you
And seek some words with that knight.
I intend to offer him guidance   3305

And whatever help I can.
I endorse both him and his cause."
      Then the king came down from the tower
And ordered his horse saddled.
Out came a huge war horse;   3310
And he set his foot in the stirrup
And mounted. He took with him
Three knights and a pair of soldiers,
Wanting no display of force.
They rode straight down the slope   3315
Until they reached the bridge,
Where they found our knight cleaning
His wounds and stopping the flow
Of blood. The king fancied
His guest would be a long time   3320
Healing—but he might as well
Have planned to dry up the sea.
The king quickly dismounted
And the badly wounded man
Immediately straightened to greet him   3325
Properly, not knowing who
This was, but showing no sign
Of the pain in his hands and feet,
Acting as if his health
Were perfect. Seeing this brave   3330
Effort, the king hurried
To greet him: "Sir, I'm astonished
To find you making such
A sudden visit to this country.
But I must tell you how welcome   3335
You are, for no one's ever
Attempted so dangerous a feat,

Requiring such incredible courage,
And no one will again.
My admiration is greater   3340
Still, believe me, for you've done
What no one has even thought
Of doing. You'll find me well
Disposed, faithful and courteous:
I am the king of this land,   3345
And I place myself completely
At your service, at your need.
And I think I know exactly
Why you're here: it's the queen,
Is it not, that you've come seeking?"   3350
"My lord, you've guessed correctly:
I've come only for the queen."
"My friend," said the king, "it won't
Be easy to achieve what you're after.
You've been badly hurt: I can see   3355
Your bloody wounds. And he
Who brought her here is truly
Ill disposed: he won't
Return her without a fight.
You need to rest, and take care   3360
Of your wounds, and be sure they're completely
Healed. We'll give you the Holy
Balm of the Three Marys,
Or anything better that exists,
For I'm deeply concerned with your care   3365
And I long for your cure. The queen
Is kept in a fine apartment,
And no one's been guilty of carnal
Abuse, not even my son,

Who brought her here. That angers   3370
Him—and there's never been
A man with so terrible a temper.
But I share your feelings, believe me,
And with God's blessing I'll help you
As much as I possibly can.   3375
My son is well equipped,
But I'll give you weapons and armor
Just as good, and the kind
Of horse you deserve, though he won't
Be pleased. And like it or not,   3380
I place you under my personal
Protection. Worry about no one
In this land, except the man
Who brought the queen to this kingdom.
In all my life I've never   3385
Quarreled with anyone as I have
With him: I almost sent him
Into exile, angry
As I was that he wouldn't return her.
He's my son, yes—but don't   3390
Worry: unless he beats you
In battle there's nothing he can do,
For I won't allow it." "I thank you,
Sir!" said our knight. "But I'm wasting
Precious time I can't   3395
Afford to lose. Let me
Assure you I haven't a thing
To complain of; these scratches don't hurt.
Bring me to your son, please:
The weapons I have are good   3400
Enough, and I'm more than ready

For the give and take of battle."
"My friend, you'd do much better
To wait two or three weeks,
And let your wounds heal.   3405
Even a rest of a week
Or two would do you good.
Nor can I permit—
I will not look on, I will not
Allow—that you go into combat   3410
Armed and equipped as you are."
"May it please you, sir," our knight
Replied, "there's nothing more
I need, to engage in battle,
Nor can I permit   3415
The slightest delay—neither
An hour, nor a minute, nor a moment.
Since you insist, however,
I will wait until tomorrow,
And to speak of a longer interval,   3420
I assure you, would waste your breath."
Then the king agreed: it would be
Exactly as he wished. He ordered
Those who'd come with him to conduct
The knight to his lodging, placing   3425
Themselves at his service, and they all
Obeyed to the last detail.
And the king, who badly wanted
A peaceful solution, if possible,
Went to his son once again.   3430
His mission was to speak for peace,
For concord, harmony, and agreement,
So he said, "Dear son, settle

This business without fighting!
This knight's not here for amusement,   3435
For bow-and-arrow contests,
Or for hunting: it's fame and glory
And reputation he's after.
What he really needs is rest,
As I've seen for myself. If he'd listen   3440
To me, he'd wait this month,
And the next one, before he'd engage
In combat, for which he hungers.
Do you honestly think returning
The queen would bring you dishonor?   3445
Then think again, my son,
For there's not the slightest chance
Of that. But keeping what isn't
Yours is against both reason
And right. He'd gladly have fought   3450
The battle right now—at once—
Though his hands and feet are in pieces,
Cut and sliced all over."
"You talk like a frightened fool,"
Said Méléagant to his father.   3455
"By the faith I owe to Saint Peter,
I'm not following *your*
Advice! Pull me apart
With horses before I listen
To you! Let him find his honor   3460
And I'll find mine. Let him hunt
For glory on his own road, and I'll
Take mine. If he's hungry for a fight,
I'm at least a hundred times hungrier!"
"Clearly, folly attracts you,"   3465

Said the king. "You'll surely find it.
Tomorrow you'll test your courage
Against his, since that's what you want."
"May nothing I do worry me
Less than that!" said the son.   3470
"I only wish it could be
Today: why wait for tomorrow?
Just see how sad my face is,
And the deep rings round my eyes!
Do you think I'm worried? grieving?   3475
Troubled? immensely afraid?
I won't be happy until
I fight him; nothing will please me."
          The king saw that nothing
Could bend or persuade him, and with great   3480
Regret left, then took
A fine, strong horse and excellent
Weapons and armor, and sent them
To him who was well acquainted
With their use, and was glad to have them.   3485
And he also sent an old, old
Man, a devout Christian
And as loyal as anyone alive,
Who was better at curing wounds
Than Montpellier's learned doctors.   3490
And all that night he labored,
As the king had directed, making
Our knight as healthy as he could.
Then the news spread, and knights
And ladies appeared, and girls   3495
And barons, from neighboring lands,
The king's people and pure

Strangers, riding rapidly
All through the long nighttime,
Hurrying from far and near   3500
To reach the king's country
By dawn. So many came,
And were packed so densely around
The great tower, that when daylight
Broke no one could move   3505
Hand or foot. And the king
Awoke at dawn, grieving
For this battle, and went to his son
Once more, finding him already
Wearing his Poitiers-crafted   3510
Helmet. He could not be stopped,
Nothing could bring him to peace,
Though the king felt obliged to try
And did his best. At the king's
Direction, the battle would be fought   3515
In front of the tower, in the center
Of the square where the great crowd
Had assembled. The king summoned
The stranger first, and our knight
Was led forth and placed   3520
Among the folk from Logres,
Who had gathered together in one spot.
Just as people came,
Year after year, at Christmas
And Pentecost, to hear   3525
The cathedral organ, the crowd
Poured into the square,
Packed as they always were.
And a host of girls from King Arthur's

Realm, fresh from three days   3530
Of fasting, had been walking barefoot
And in woolen hair shirts, in order
To invoke the force and power
Of God for our knight against
His enemy, in fighting this battle,   3535
As he was, for all the foreign
Prisoners. And the people of that country,
For their part, prayed for their prince,
Begging God to give him
Victory and honor. Soon   3540
After dawn, before morning
Prayers, the knights were led
To the field of battle, both
Mounted on horses wearing
Protective armor. The prince   3545
Was a well-built, noble-looking
And handsome man, his hammered
Mail shirt beautifully fitted,
His helmet and the shield hung
From his neck perfectly matching.   3550
But even those who supported
His cause preferred the knight
Of the cart, all agreeing
That Méléagant was nothing
In comparison. They waited, there   3555
In the center of the square, as the king
Joined them, determined to try
This one last time, to arrange
For peace. But he could not persuade
His son. "Rein in your horses   3560
With both hands," he said,

"Till I reach the top of the tower.
That's hardly too much to ask;
You can easily wait that long."
Almost trembling, he left them,   3565
And immediately went to where
He knew he would find the queen,
Who had begged him, the night before,
To place her in a spot from which
She could watch the entire battle,   3570
And having granted her wish
He went, now, to honor
His word and, forever courteous,
Bring her there himself.
So he set her at a high window,   3575
Then seated himself to her right,
Also at a window. And all
Around them were many notable
Knights and ladies, some
From the king's country, some   3580
From Logres, and native-born girls,
And others from among the prisoners,
The latter extremely active
At their prayers and invocations,
As all the captive men   3585
And women were, on their knight's
Behalf, looking to God
And to him for their final deliverance.
And then the combatants, freed
For their fight, ordered the crowd   3590
To withdraw, set their shields
In place, their arms through the straps,
And, aiming their spears, dashed

At each other, striking so fiercely
That the points went two arms deep,   3595
And the shields split and shattered
To bits. Their horses, too,
Came smashing breastplate into
Breastplate, with incredible force,
And the crashing shock of shields   3600
And helmets, horses and men,
Sounded for all the world
Like a towering clap of thunder,
And every strap and belt
And spur and rein and girth   3605
Broke, and even the heavy
Saddles snapped at the bow,
And neither knight was shamed
Or surprised to be tossed to the ground,
As everything underneath him   3610
Gave way. They leaped to their feet
And continued the combat like a pair
Of wild boars, not bothering with insults
Or boasts, but striking each other
With heavy blows of their steel   3615
Swords, like men who violently
Hate one another. Their slashing
Strokes often cut
Through helmets and mail shirts, making
Blood spurt from the metal.   3620
They fought savagely, giving
And taking mighty blows,
Cruel and heavy. Each
Assaulted the other on equal
Terms, neither able   3625

To gain the slightest advantage.
But it could not last: he
Who had crossed the Sword Bridge was surely
Weakened by all his wounds,
As everyone watching knew,   3630
And those who favored that knight
Were terribly worried, seeing
His strokes weaken, sensing
Him getting the worst, afraid
That Méléagant would seize   3635
The upper hand and victory
Would be his. A buzzing murmur
Ran through the crowd. But up
In the tower, at a window, a wise
Girl was watching, and she thought   3640
To herself the knight most certainly
Wasn't fighting so terrible
A battle for her, nor
For anyone standing in the crowd
Of ordinary people,   3645
But strictly and solely for the queen
And no one else—and if
He knew she was at a window,
Watching from on high, it might give him
Strength and courage. And had she   3650
Known his name, she'd have gladly
Told him (calling down
From the tower) that his love was there,
And he could glance up, and see her.
So she hurried to the queen and said,   3655
"My lady, in the name of God,
For your sake and ours, please,

Tell me that knight's name,
If you know it, so I can offer him
Help." "Young lady," said the queen,   3660
"Your request, it seems to me,
Contains nothing in any way
Hateful or wicked, but only
Concern for his good. As long
As I've known him, this knight's name   3665
Has been Lancelot of the Lake."
"Oh God!" said the girl. "How my happy
Heart is leaping with joy!"
Then she jumped to the window and shouted,
As loud as she could, in a voice   3670
That everyone heard: "Lancelot!
Turn your head up and look—
See who's here, watching!"

     As soon as he heard his name,
Lancelot turned and looked   3675
Behind him, and saw, seated
High at an open window,
What more than anything else
In the world he wanted to see.
And then, from the moment he saw her,   3680
He neither moved his head
Nor looked in any other
Direction, fighting with his back
To his enemy, and Méléagant
Immediately began to press him   3685
As hard as he could, delighted
To think that, now, the knight
Could no longer face him and defend
Himself. And his countrymen, too,

Were delighted, while the men of Logres   3690
Were so sick at heart they could not
Stand, many falling
To their knees, but many fainting
Away, stretched on the ground.
Sorrow and excitement were everywhere.   3695
But the girl, high at her window,
Shouted down once more:
"Ah, Lancelot! Can you really
Be as stupid as you look?
You seemed to be all   3700
That a knight should be, till now:
You had me convinced that God
Had never made a knight
Who could challenge you for courage
And strength and virtue. And now   3705
We see you fighting backwards,
Looking away from your enemy!
Do your fighting with your face
Turned to this tower, so you'll see her
Better! Let her shine on you!"   3710
Outraged at the insult, and deeply
Shamed, Lancelot bitterly
Cursed himself for letting
The combat go against him,
Here in the sight of them all.   3715
With a leap, he drove behind
Méléagant, forcing
His enemy to stand with his back
To the tower. Méléagant
Struggled to regain his ground,   3720
But Lancelot charged him, striking

So many powerful strokes,
Swinging with all his strength,
That he forced a further retreat,
Two or three unwilling,   3725
Unwelcome steps. Between
The strength Love had lent him,
Offered in willing assistance,
And the hate swelling in his heart
As the battle wore on, all   3730
His powers and quickness had returned.
Love and his mortal hate—
Fiercer than any ever
Known—combined to make him
So fearsome that Méléagant   3735
Was suddenly afraid,
For never in all his life
Had an enemy seemed so strong,
Or pressed and hurt him so badly
As this knight was doing. He tried   3740
As hard as he could to keep him
At a distance, feinting, ducking,
Bobbing, badly hurt
Each time he was hit. Lancelot
Wasted no breath on threats,   3745
Kept driving him toward the tower
And the queen, over and over
Coming as close as he could,
Forcing Méléagant back,
Each time, barely a foot   3750
Away from stepping out
Of her sight. So Lancelot led him
Up and down, this way

And that, always making him
Stop in front of his lady,   3755
The queen, who'd set his heart
On fire, just knowing she was
Watching—a fiercely roaring,
Burning-hot flame impelling him
Straight at Méléagant   3760
And pushing his helpless enemy
Forward and back like a cripple,
Tugging him along like a blind man
Or a beggar at the end of a rope.
The king saw his son   3765
Utterly overwhelmed
And was filled with pity and compassion:
He had to help, if he could.
But the queen, he knew, was the only
Possible source of assistance,   3770
So he turned to her and spoke:
"Lady, for as long as you've been
In my land you've had my love
And honor; I've served you well,
And always gladly, in every   3775
Way I could. Let me
Ask you, now, to repay me.
And the gift I ask you to give me
Could only be granted out
Of the purest love. I can see   3780
Quite well—there's not the slightest
Doubt—that my son has lost
This battle. And I speak to you, now,
Not on this score, but because
It's clear that Lancelot   3785

Could easily kill him, if he chose to.
I hope you want that no more
Than I do—not that my son
Has treated you well—he hasn't—
But simply because I beg you   3790
For your mercy. Let him live.
Let the final blow be withheld.
And thus you can tell me, if you choose,
How you value the honor
I've shown you." "Dear sir, if that's   3795
What you want, I want it, too.
I certainly hate and loathe
Your son, for the best of reasons,
But you indeed have served me
So well that it pleases me   3800
To please you by stopping the battle."
They had not whispered private
Words; both Lancelot
And Méléagant heard them.
Lovers are obedient men,   3805
Cheerfully willing to do
Whatever the beloved, who holds
Their entire heart, desires.
Lancelot had no choice,
For if ever anyone loved   3810
More truly than Pyramus
It was him. Hearing her response,
As soon as the final word
Fell from her mouth, declaring,
"Dear sir, if you want the battle   3815
Stopped, I want that, too,"
Nothing in the world could have made him

Fight, or even move,
No matter if it cost his life.
He stood as still as a stone—   3820
But Méléagant struck
As hard as he could, angry
And shamed to find himself
The object of anyone's pity.
The king came hurrying down   3825
From the tower, to stop him. Straight
To the field of battle he went,
Speaking these words to his son:
"What's this? You think it's fine
To go on fighting, after   3830
He's stopped? You act like a savage!
It's far too late for heroics:
Everyone knows he's won,
Everyone knows you've been beaten!"
Out of his mind with shame,   3835
Méléagant denied
Defeat: "Have you gone blind?
There's something wrong with your eyes!
Anyone who thinks I've been beaten
Is surely as blind as a bat!"   3840
"Who do you think believes you?"
Said the king. "All these people
Can tell for themselves what's true
And false. We know you're lying."
And the king ordered his men   3845
To take his son away.
It was done at once, exactly
As the king commanded. Against
His wishes, Méléagant

Was removed. But Lancelot   3850
Left of his own free will,
For he would have stood without fighting
Even if the prince had hurt him.
And the king said to his son,
"As God is my witness, you'll now   3855
Make peace and give up the queen!
This quarrel's completely finished.
It's over, it's done with: that's all!"
"What stupid things you're saying,"
Said his son. "You're making no sense.   3860
Go! Just let us fight;
Stop meddling where no one wants you."
But the king insisted it was settled:
"You'd clearly be dead, if I'd let
This battle continue." "He   3865
Kill me? He's the one
Who'd be dead, and I'd be the victor,
If you hadn't interfered:
If only you hadn't stopped us!"
"God save me," said the king,   3870
"You're simply wasting your breath."
"Why?" "Because I say so.
Your stupid pride would kill you,
If I let you do what you want.
Only a fool could long   3875
For death: you understand nothing!
I know you hate me for trying
To save your life. But God
Won't let me watch you die—
Not if I can help it!   3880
I couldn't bear the pain."

He talked and argued, argued
And talked, till peace was arranged.
And the terms of their accord
Gave Lancelot the queen   3885
But Méléagant the unquestioned
Right, for a year to come,
To call for another combat,
Man to man, where
And when he wanted. That combat   3890
Did not concern our knight.
The peace pleased everyone,
And the court of King Arthur, ruler
Of Britain and Cornwall, was chosen
As the site of that future battle.   3895
So much was settled—but still
The queen, and Lancelot with her,
Had to agree that should
The second battle be won
By Méléagant, she   3900
Would return with him, without
Opposition. The queen gave
Her consent, and Lancelot, too.
And then it was truly over,
And both knights disarmed.   3905
        It was the custom, in that country,
That once anyone left it
Everyone else could leave,
If they wished. They all blessed
Our knight, nor do I need   3910
To tell you how happy they were—
Indeed, they were overjoyed!
All the strangers in that strange

Land gathered around him,
Voicing their profound pleasure: 3915
"Sir, we were thrilled the moment
We heard your name, knowing
That if it was you who came
To free us, we'd certainly be freed."
And in their joy they crowded   3920
Around him, all of them anxious
To push in close and touch him.
And those whose hands could reach him
Were happier than words can express.
But despite the prisoners' ecstatic   3925
Joy, there were also those
Who suffered and could not rejoice:
Méléagant and his men
Had nothing to celebrate;
They were silent, and thoughtful, and glum.   3930
The king had left the field,
Leading Lancelot with him,
And Lancelot asked to be taken
To the queen. "And how could I
Object?" said the king. "Of course   3935
You'd like to see her. Indeed,
If you wish you can also see
Sir Kay." Lancelot almost
Fell to his knees with delight.
The king took him directly   3940
To the great hall, where the queen
Had been waiting for our knight to appear.
       Seeing Bademagu
Hand in hand with Lancelot,
She rose to greet the king,   3945

Seeming greatly embarrassed:
Head down, she stood there, silent.
"Lady, I bring you Lancelot,"
Said the king, "who's come to see you.
I'm sure his visit will please you."   3950
"Me?" she answered. "How could it?
I've nothing to do with his coming."
"Good Lord, lady!" said the king,
An exceedingly courteous man,
"How can you say such a thing —   3955
Mistreating a man who's served you
So wonderfully well, often
Putting his life at risk
And all for you? A man
Who came to your aid and fought with   3960
My son solely for your sake,
Obliging him to surrender
What he never wanted to lose?"
"My lord, truly, he's wasted
His time. I can't help it: 3965
I take no pleasure in his sight."
And Lancelot stood there, thinking,
Then replied with infinite courtesy,
As a true lover should,
"You leave me sorrowful, lady,   3970
But I dare not ask you why."
        He could have complained, and bitterly,
Had she been willing to listen,
But as if to make him feel worse
She spoke not a word, just walking   3975
Away to another room.
Lancelot's eyes, and his heart

As well, followed her out.
It seemed to him far
Too quick, far too short   3980
A trip: his eyes would have followed
Her in, if they possibly could.
His noble heart, which beat
With greater strength and power,
Crossed the threshold with her   3985
And went in, as she shut the door,
Though his eyes, all filled with tears,
Remained outside with his body.
Then the king took him aside,
Whispering, "But Lancelot,   3990
What can she mean, refusing
To see you, not saying a word?
Surely, if you used to speak,
You two, she shouldn't be
Capricious and ignore you this way—   3995
Not with all you've done
For her! Tell me, if you know,
Why would she treat you like this?
What have you done to deserve it?"
"My lord, I had no warning.   4000
But clearly she took no pleasure
In seeing my face or hearing
My words, and it weighs on my heart."
"By God," said the king, "she's behaving
Badly. You've risked your life,   4005
And all for her! But come,
My good sweet friend, it's time
You had a word with Sir Kay."
"Gladly," was the answer. "I'd like that."

The king led him to Sir Kay,   4010
And seeing Lancelot there
In front of him, the steward's
First words were: "Lord! How
You've put me to shame!" "I have?"
Replied our knight. "Explain   4015
Yourself. How have I shamed you?"
"You couldn't have shamed me more,
Doing so easily what I
Could never do at all."
      And then the king left   4020
The room, and they were alone,
And Lancelot asked Sir Kay
How bad his suffering had been.
"It's never ended," he said,
"And now it's worse than before.   4025
Over and over I was sure
I was dead, and so I'd have been
Except for the king, who showed me
Sweet compassion and friendship.
Whenever he heard I needed   4030
Anything, he always arranged
Whatever was wanted. He never
Failed me, but acted at once,
The moment he learned of my pain.
He was always ready to help,   4035
But Méléagant, his son,
Was completely different, evil,
Treacherous, secretly ordering
The doctors to bind my wounds
With mortal poisons instead   4040
Of healing balms. The king

Was a true father, the other
A false one. The king brought me
Medicines and cures;
His son, like a stepfather, did his wicked   4045
Secret best to kill me,
Taking away his father's
Blessed gifts, replacing
Good with evil. He wished
To see me die. But his father   4050
The king was not aware
Of what his son was doing:
He wouldn't have allowed such cruel
And traitorous, such murderous acts!
You can't imagine how generous   4055
He's been to my lady, the queen.
Since Noah built his ark
There's never been a better
Sentinel, guarding a frontier
Tower; he's stood at the door,   4060
Denying entrance even
To his son, who was bitterly resentful,
Except when crowds were present
Or the king himself could be there.
This noble king has shown her,   4065
And continues to show her, all
The respect our gracious queen
Deserves and is able to command.
She herself, and only
She, has laid out the rules,   4070
And the king could not have more
Admired and approved her conduct.
But tell me: can it be true,

but he didn't stop his son from taking her

As they say, that Guinevere
Publicly expressed such anger   4075
Toward you that she wouldn't speak
A word?" "It's true," was the answer,
"Absolutely true.
Have you any idea, in the name
Of God, why she should hate me?"   4080
Sir Kay said he did not,
But thought it exceedingly strange.
"Let it be as she wishes!"
Was all Lancelot could say,
Adding, "It's time I left,   4085
And went in search of Gawain,
Who also came to this land:
He and I agreed
To meet at the Sunken Bridge."
And so, leaving Kay's room,   4090
He came to the king and asked
Permission to go on his way.
And the king granted him leave.
But those he'd set free and released
From their prison clamored to come   4095
Along. And Lancelot said,
"If you wish to come with me
You may certainly come. But if
You wish to stay with the queen
You're equally free to remain.   4100
No one needs to leave."
So all who wished to depart
Joined him, delighted to be going.
But all the girls stayed
With the queen, happy to have   4105

A choice, and ladies stayed,
And some knights, but none who desperately
Longed to return and could not
Wait any longer. And those
Who remained did so for the queen,   4110
Who'd announced she was waiting for Gawain
And would not move until
News of him should arrive.
       The news was quickly spread:
The queen was free, and all   4115
The others with her; any
Who wished to leave could go
When and as they pleased.
Former prisoners went up
And down, all asking each other,   4120
All discussing the same
Subject, none of them sad
To see the old control posts
Demolished: things had changed
So much, they could come and go   4125
As they liked! But when those who lived
In that country heard how the combat
Had gone, that Lancelot had won,
Hordes of them hurried down
To the road he would have to follow,   4130
Believing the king would be pleased
If they captured this foreign knight
And brought him back as a prisoner.
All those with him were unarmed
And utterly helpless against   4135
The men who now surrounded them:
No wonder Lancelot

Was quickly captured and disarmed,
And led back, his feet tied
Together under his horse's   4140
Belly. "No, no," the former
Prisoners protested, "the king
Himself has guaranteed
Our passage!" "We know nothing about it,"
They were answered. "But having been captured   4145
You'll come with us to court."
A rumor soon reached the king's
Ears that his people had captured
Lancelot and killed him. Hearing
This news, the king was deeply   4150
Upset, and swore that whoever
Had done this should die at once,
Without defense or delay;
The only choice they could have,
Once he'd caught them, would be   4155
Between hanging, burning,
Or drowning. If they tried to deny it
He wouldn't believe a word,
For he'd been struck to the heart,
And the pain was immense—and the shame   4160
That would fall on him, if he failed
To avenge this death, would be even
Greater—but he would avenge it!
          The rumor ran in every
Direction, reaching the queen   4165
As she sat down to eat,
And the false news of Lancelot's
Death came close to killing
Her as well, for she

Took it for truth, and the shock   4170
Was so intense her lips
Almost forgot how to speak,
But because of those around her
She said, "This death is horribly
Painful—and I *should* be grieved,   4175
Since he came to this country for me.
He deserves my pain and my grief."
And then she said to herself,
Softly and unheard, that eating
And drinking had now become   4180
Impossible, if indeed he
Whose life gave meaning to her own
Was truly dead. Slowly
And sadly, she rose from the table,
Already mourning in so silent   4185
A voice that no one could hear her.
And feeling driven to kill
Herself, she clutched at her throat,
Silently confessing, first,
That she alone was at fault,   4190
Accusing herself of sinful
Behavior, of wicked acts
Directed at the man whose heart
Had always been hers, and still
Would be hers, were he still alive.   4195
And knowing she'd been so cruel
Stole away her beauty.
The thought of such wickedness drained
And discolored her skin more
Than fasting or all-night vigils.   4200
All the evil she'd done

Flooded her mind, bit
By bit; she remembered it all
And cried, "Oh God! What
Was I thinking, when my lover appeared,   4205
Not showing him my pleasure,
Refusing to allow him a word?
To deny him every attention
Was absolutely mad!
Mad? Better, by God,   4210
To call me cruel, and a traitress.
It was only a joke, a whim,
But he took it deeply to heart
And never forgave me. I know it,
It was I who killed him, who gave him   4215
The mortal blow: I know it!
He came to me, laughing with joy,
Believing I would return
His pleasure, rejoice at his sight—
And I refused to see him: 4220
Could I have dealt him a blow
More mortal? Denying him even
A word was like cutting out
His heart and killing him, then
And there. And so I killed him: 4225
Why hunt for other assassins?
Oh God! Can I ever redeem
This murder, this mortal sin?
No—not unless
All the rivers stop running   4230
And the sea goes dry. Lord,
How good it would be, once—
Just once—before I die,

Were he wrapped in my arms again!
How? Why, both of us naked;   4235
That's when I'd be the happiest.
But since he's dead, to go on
Living would simply be wicked.
And why? To be alive
After he's dead: would that   4240
Injure my beloved—nothing
To delight in except my sorrow?
And yet how sweet that sorrow
Would be, had he been able
To see it when he was alive.   4245
Would it not be wicked
To prefer death to such suffering?
Living as long as I can,
And enduring this pain, will be pleasure
Enough: I should live and suffer,   4250
Not die and be at peace."
The queen was in mourning for two
Whole days, not eating or drinking,
And everyone thought she was dead.
The world is full of people   4255
Just waiting to bring us bad news,
And one of them came to Lancelot,
Announcing his lady's death.
His heart was utterly broken;
No one could doubt how grief   4260
And sorrow overwhelmed him.
Indeed, to tell you the truth,
If you really want to know:
He had no interest in living;
Death was all he wanted.   4265

But before he killed himself—
Pulling off his belt
And tying a fatal knot
At the end—weeping as he spoke
He declared, "Death! What a forfeit   4270
You've taken, turning health
Into sickness! I've fallen sick,
But with no disease except sorrow.
And yet this sorrow is mortal.
Fine: I hope it proves fatal,   4275
And Death will allow me to die.
Indeed? Is death denied me,
Except when Death wills it?
Fine—as long as he lets me
Tie this knot around   4280
My neck, forcing Death
To take me, like it or not.
Death prefers victims
Anxious to keep him away.
I'll pull him in with my belt,   4285
Catch him and make him come,
And once I've got him, I'll keep him,
Compel him to please me. The problem,
Clearly, is how slowly he comes,
And how much I wish he'd hurry!"   4290
He moved quickly from words
To actions, putting his head
In the noose, with the knot at his neck,
And determined to die at once,
Wound the other end   4295
Of the belt around the bow
Of his saddle, letting no one

See, then dropped to the ground,
Intending his horse to drag him
Along until he strangled.   4300
He refused to live any longer.
Seeing him fall, those
Who were riding with him thought
He might have fainted, for none of them
Noticed the noose knotted   4305
Around his neck. Quickly,
They bent and pulled him up,
Their arms clasped about him—
And saw, only then,
How he'd made the leather his enemy,   4310
Knotting it round his neck.
They cut it off at once,
But the noose had so constricted
His throat that it took time
Before he could speak, the veins   4315
All up and down his neck
Close to breaking. And then,
No matter how much he might want to,
He could no longer harm himself.
But how it hurt that they watched him!   4320
He fairly burned with fury
And regret, wanting only
To die, if only they'd let him.
They would not, and he could not, so he said
To himself, "Ah Death! You disgusting   4325
Old fraud, how much are you worth
If you haven't the strength or the will
To take me instead of my lady?
Perhaps it's too good a deed,

And *that's* why you wouldn't do it!   4330
That must be the answer: you spared me
Like a thief and a traitor! Ha!
Such respect and kindness!
How well you planned your moves!
I'll see you in Hell before   4335
I thank you for favors like this!
I can't even say who
I hate most—Life,
For keeping me, or Death, who won't
Kill me. You're both against me.   4340
And yet it's right, by God,
That wanting to die, I'm alive,
For I should have killed myself
The moment my lady the queen
Showed how deeply she hates me.   4345
There's got to be some reason;
She wouldn't have done it for nothing—
And yet I can't understand.
For had I known what was wrong
I'd have moved heaven and earth   4350
To amend it, however she liked,
Before her soul was called
To God, if only she'd shown me
Some mercy. Oh Lord: what
Did I do? She'd probably heard   4355
How I'd ridden in the cart.
Yet how could she blame me for that?
But what else could it be? It was that.
Still, if the cart caused her
To hate me, how could Love   4360
Allow it? How little Love

Must be understood, to turn
Such a thing against me. Nothing
Done in the name of Love
Can be held against a lover: 4365
Whatever a lover does
For love is love, and is right.
Did I do it only for my love?
Oh Lord, what can I say!
Can I still call her my love?   4370
Do I dare use that word?
All I know of love
Insists that, if she loved me,
She shouldn't have been repelled
But loved me even more,   4375
For doing what Love requires
Strikes me as honoring Love,
No matter if it's riding in a cart.
She should have known it was done
For Love, had she seen it correctly.   4380
That's how lovers are tested
By Love, and how Love knows them
As hers. But my lady didn't like
What I did: she more than proved
That dislike with her cold greeting.   4385
And just the same, for doing
This deed her lover has been showered
With shame, and reproach, many times
Over, and accepted it gladly,
Though it soured what I meant to be sweet,   4390
For those who know nothing of Love,
By God, are always acting
That way, washing honor

With shame, though honor's not cleansed
By such a bath, but soiled.   4395
Those who know nothing of Love
Constantly treat it badly,
Unafraid of its laws,
Pure pagans without belief.
But those who obey Love's orders   4400
Achieve honor and glory,
Forgiven for whatever they do,
While those who fail it are cowards."
    And so Lancelot lamented,
And his men rode sadly along   4405
Beside him, guarding their lord.
Then after a time, new news
Arrived: the queen was not dead!
And the knight was himself again:
However profoundly, and long,   4410
He'd mourned her death, now
He celebrated her life
A thousand times more strongly.
By the time he'd come as close
As eight or nine miles to King   4415
Bademagu's castle,
The king too heard news
That cheered him immensely: the knight
Was safe and sound and would soon
Be with him again. Like the courteous,   4420
Noble gentleman he was,
The king hurried to tell
The queen, who said, "Your majesty,
Since you bear this news, I believe it.
But had he truly been dead,   4425

I'd never have been happy again.
All the pleasure in life
Would be gone, had a knight died
In my service and on my account."
          And then the king left her,   4430
And she waited, and waited, impatient
For her love and her joy to return.
Continuing any quarrel
With him was the last thing on her mind!
But the rumor that came to her ears   4435
Over and over, never
At rest, was that Lancelot
Would have killed himself for her,
And had tried, but they would not let him.
She believed it, and was thrilled at the thought,   4440
But nothing in the world could have made her
Want such a total disaster.
And finally, having hurried
As fast as he could, he came.
The moment the king saw him   4445
He ran and hugged and kissed him,
Feeling so light with joy
He should have been able to fly.
But seeing those who had captured
And bound the knight, his joy   4450
Ended: they'd ridden hard,
He said, to reach their own death.
They answered that whatever they'd done
Had been meant to honor the king's
Wishes. "It may have pleased you!"   4455
Said the king, "But not me. It had nothing
To do with this knight, who was under

My protection. The shame's
Not his, but mine, only
Mine. And you'll pay for your pleasure!"   4460
        Seeing Bademagu's
Fury, Lancelot sought
To calm him, and bring about peace,
And after working long
And hard, succeeded. Then the king   4465
Brought him to see the queen.
And now her eyes were not
Lowered to the ground, she came
To greet him gaily, offering
All the honor she knew how   4470
To give, making him sit
At her side. And they talked
Of whatever came to their minds,
Neither of them hunting for words,
For Love supplied them in abundance.   4475
And seeing how well it went,
And nothing he said displeased
The queen, Lancelot lowered
His voice: "Lady," he said,
"I was taken aback at the greeting   4480
You gave me, the other day,
Not saying a single word.
I felt myself close to death
And had not the courage, as I have
Today, to say a word   4485
Or ask you why. Lady,
If you'll tell me what I've done
To deserve such torment, I'm ready,
Now, to make you amends."

To which the queen answered,   4490
"Indeed? Didn't the cart
Shame you the least little bit?
You must have hesitated,
For you lingered a good two steps.
And that, you see, was my sole   4495
Reason for ignoring your presence."
"May God keep me from another
Such error," said Lancelot,
"And may He show me no mercy
If you haven't spoken the truth!   4500
In the name of God, Lady,
Tell me what I must do
To earn your forgiveness, and whatever
It is I will do it at once.
I beg you: pardon my fault."   4505
"My friend," said the queen gaily,
"Your fault is freely forgiven.
You have my absolute pardon."
"I thank you, Lady," he said.
"But I cannot tell you, here,   4510
All I would like to say.
I'd be grateful for the chance to speak
In private, if that can be managed."
Then the queen motioned—not
With her hand, but her eyes—to a window,   4515
And said, "Come speak to me
Tonight, at that window, when everyone
Else will be asleep.
Come by way of that orchard.
I can't let you in,   4520
Nor can you stay the night.

I shall have to stay inside,
And you will have to stay out.
I won't be able to touch you,
Except with my hand, or my mouth.   4525
But if it gives you pleasure
I'll stay there till dawn, for love
Of you. We cannot come
Together, for Sir Kay, the steward,
Sleeps on a bed in my room,   4530
Still sick from the wounds he received.
And the door is always closed,
And it's strong, and very well guarded.
Be very careful, when you come,
That none of those watching see you."   4535
"Lady," he said, "If I can,
No one will see me, and neither
Think nor say an evil
Word." And thus they talked,
And parted wonderfully happy.   4540
      Lancelot left her, his spirits
So high that all his pains
And sorrows had been forgotten.
But night was too slow in coming,
And the day lingered too long: 4545
It seemed to him a hundred
Days, or even a year.
He'd hurry to their rendezvous,
If only night would come!
Then finally the thick, dark   4550
Night fought the day
To its knees and slowly covered it
Over with its heavy cloak.

And seeing the light fade,
He pretended an immense fatigue,   4555
Saying he'd been awake
Too long, and needed to rest.
You who've used the same trick
Don't need to have it explained:
He made a great show of weariness   4560
And took himself off to bed—
But found no comfort, for sleep
Was not what he had in mind.
He could not have slept, nor would he
Have dared to even had he wanted   4565
To try. And soon he rose,
Quietly, not a bit unhappy
That no moon was shining, and no stars,
And all through the house not a candle
Or a lamp or a lantern was lit.   4570
He slipped outdoors, careful
That no one was watching; everyone
Thought he was fast asleep,
Lost in his bed for the night.
No one went with him, or showed him   4575
The path, as he went to the orchard,
And he met no one on the way.
And his luck held: part
Of the wall around the orchard
Had recently fallen, and through   4580
The hole he went, quickly,
And stood beneath the window,
Still as a stone, careful
Not to cough or sneeze.
And then the queen appeared,   4585

Dressed in a snow-white gown.
She wore neither a coat
Nor any covering but a short
Red cloak, fur-trimmed, across
Her shoulders. Seeing the queen   4590
Bend her head against
The window's great iron bars,
Lancelot greeted her with gentle
Warmth, which she returned,
Immense longing gripping   4595
Them both, each for the other.
No harsh or angry words
Passed between them: pressing
As close as they could, they were just
Able to clasp hand   4600
To hand. How it hurt them,
Unable to be together,
And how they cursed those iron
Bars! But Lancelot assured her,
Should she be willing, he'd come   4605
And join her: no iron bars
Could keep him out! The queen
Quickly replied, "Can't
You see? This iron's too thick
To bend, too strong to break.   4610
Please: don't even attempt it!
How could you possibly pull
Away a single one?"
"Ah, don't worry, my lady!
No iron can keep me out.   4615
Nothing can stop me from coming
To you, if you want me to come.

Just say the word, and consider it
As good as done. Your
Not wanting me in is the only   4620
Obstacle that could keep me out,
The only barrier I can't
Break down." "I want you in,"
Said the queen. "That's not the question.
But let me quickly return   4625
To bed, and lie there, and watch,
Because it won't be pleasant
Or at all amusing if my husband's
Steward, who's sleeping here,
Hears you at work, and wakes up.   4630
Besides, it's better for me
To be back in bed, not standing
Here for everyone to see."
"Go back to bed, lady,
But have no fear: this   4635
Is work I can do quietly.
These bars will come out quickly
And with hardly an effort, and no one
Will hear me or know what I've done."
        The queen hurried back   4640
To her bed, and the knight prepared
To pull the window apart.
Taking hold of the bars,
He bent them toward him until
They snapped away from their sockets.   4645
But the iron edge was so sharp
It cut through his little
Finger, down to the bone,
And sliced deep in the knuckle

Of the finger next to it. He had no   4650
Awareness of the blood running out,
Nor the wounds; he felt no pain,
His mind on other matters.
The window was high in the wall,
But Lancelot had no trouble   4655
Climbing quickly through.
Finding Sir Kay asleep,
He approached the queen's bed,
Bowing in adoration
Before the holiest relic   4660
He knew, and the queen reached out
Her arms and drew him down,
Holding him tight against
Her breast, making the knight
As welcome in her bed, and as happy,   4665
As she possibly could, impelled
By the power of Love, and her own
Heart. It was Love that moved her,
And she loved him truly, but he
Loved her a hundred thousand   4670
Times more, for if other hearts
Had escaped Love, his
Had not. His heart was so
Completely captured that the image
Of Love in all other hearts   4675
Was a pale one. And the knight had
What he wanted, for the queen willingly
Gave him all the pleasures
Of herself, held him in her arms
As he was holding her.   4680
It was so exceedingly sweet

And good—the kisses, the embraces—
That Lancelot knew a delight
So fine, so wondrous, that no one
In the world had ever before   4685
Known anything like it, so help me
God! And that's all I'm allowed
To tell you; I can say no more.
These pleasures I'm forbidden to report
Were the most wonderful known,   4690
The most delightful. That night,
And all night long, Lancelot
Experienced incredible joy.
But the dawn came, against
His will, and he had to leave.   4695
Rising from her bed was like
Some terrible martyrdom;
He suffered immense pain.
His heart kept yearning back
To where the queen was lying,   4700
Nor could he keep it in his breast,
For after such joy he had
No heart to take away with him:
The body might go, but the heart
Would remain. He turned and went   4705
To the window—but some of him stayed,
For the curtains were spotted and stained
With the blood he'd shed as he entered.
He left more slowly than he'd come,
With much sighing and many   4710
Tears. They could plan for nothing
More, no matter how much
They longed to: reluctant to leave,

He left, and hated to go.
His hands had been badly wounded,   4715
His fingers were scarred, but he bent
The bars back where they'd been,
Set them in their sockets again,
So no matter how or where
One looked, top or bottom,   4720
Inside or out, they seemed
Completely undisturbed.
And as he passed through the window
He bowed and crossed himself,
As if acknowledging   4725
An altar. And so he left,
Sadly, seen by no one,
And returned to his lodgings. He lay down
In his bed, naked; no one
Was disturbed, no one woke up.   4730
And then he noticed, astonished,
How badly his fingers had been hurt,
But was not bothered, quite sure
That in bending the window's iron
Bars he must have cut   4735
And bruised himself. He felt
No regret: he'd rather let
Both his arms be ripped
From his body than never have gone
Through that window—though the wounds were so   4740
Severe that suffering such injuries
On some other occasion, in some other
Cause, would have been an affliction.
        Behind the closed curtains
In her room, the queen sweetly   4745

Slept the morning away,
Paying no attention
To all the bloodstained spots,
Sure the curtains were as white
And lovely as they'd always been.   4750
But Méléagant, as soon
As he'd left his bed, and was dressed,
Decided to pay a visit
To the room where the queen was lying.
He found her awake, and saw   4755
The curtains freshly spotted
With blood. Nudging his followers
With an elbow, as if hot on the trail
Of evil, he turned to Sir Kay
And saw blood spots all over   4760
His bed (for as the steward
Slept, that night, his wounds
Had opened). "Lady," he exclaimed,
"Here's the proof I've been wanting!
Trying to keep a woman   4765
Honest is truly work
For a fool, and a waste of time:
When someone's watching she slips
Away faster than when no one
Cares! And my father gave you   4770
A guard to save you from me!
That kept me out, all right—
But Sir Steward, lying right here,
Managed to find you, last night,
And took whatever he wanted.   4775
That's perfectly clear: just look!"
"At what?" she said. "The blood

On your curtains cries out against you.
I won't go into details.
But I see what I see: blood   4780
From his wounds spattered all over
Your curtains, and all over his bed.
Could one ask for better proof?"
And then, for the very first time,
The queen saw the spattered   4785
Curtains, and the bed, and was stunned;
Shame brought the color
To her face: "So help me God,
But this blood I see on my curtains
Never came from Sir Kay.   4790
Last night I had a nose bleed—
And this, I expect, is the cause."
And she really thought it was true.
"So help me," said Méléagant,
"You're babbling absolute nonsense.   4795
These empty words are worthless:
You're guilty beyond a doubt,
The truth is perfectly clear."
And then, speaking to his father's
Guards, he said, "Don't move.   4800
Keep everything just as it is,
Let no one touch this bed.
I intend to demand justice
From the king, as soon as he's seen it."
And then he sought out the king   4805
And threw himself at his feet,
"My lord, come see what you never
Suspected. Come see this queen
You've sheltered, and behold the amazing

Things I found in her chambers   4810
And have seen for myself. But first,
Before you go, I pray you
Not to forget what's mine
By justice and right. You know
As well as anyone what I risked   4815
For this woman's sake, making
You my enemy. You kept her
Guarded against me. I went
To see her, this morning, as she lay
In bed, and saw without   4820
The slightest doubt that she'd spent
The night with Sir Kay. In the name
Of God, my lord, don't
Be angry that I've come complaining
And in sorrow, for in sleeping with Kay   4825
She's shown me immense disdain
And flagrantly flaunted her hatred!"
"Be quiet!" said the king. "This is nonsense."
"My lord, come see her curtains,
And how Kay left them. Since   4830
You refuse to believe me, and insist
I'm telling you lies, let
Those curtains, and the blood from Kay's
Wounds, convince you of the truth."
"Let's go, then!" declared the king.   4835
"My eyes have never told me
Lies: I want them to see
For themselves." He hurried to the queen's
Chamber, and found her there,
Newly risen from her bed.   4840
He saw the bloody curtains

And the blood on Sir Kay's bed.
"Lady," he said, "Alas!
I see what my son has told me
Is true." "By God," she replied,   4845
"No one has ever concocted
Such a wicked lie, not even
In a dream! Sir Kay, King Arthur's
Steward, is too honest and loyal
A man to accuse of such things.   4850
And I, I don't sell
My body to the highest bidder.
Believe me, such infamy
Would never have crossed Kay's mind,
And it never, ever, occurred   4855
To me, nor would I have done it."
"My lord," said Méléagant
To his father, "how pleasant it would be
If Kay paid for his crime,
And the queen was properly shamed.   4860
Justice awaits your word:
Give it, I beg you. This false
Steward, in whom King Arthur
Placed such trust that he let him
Guard the queen, his dearest   4865
Love, has betrayed his lord."
"My lord," said Kay, "let me
Answer, and defend myself.
When I leave this world may God
Refuse my soul forgiveness   4870
If I took my pleasure of my lady!
I'd rather—much rather!—be dead
Than be guilty of such an outrageous

Crime against my lord!
May God on high not give me   4875
Back my health—let him
Take me, here and now,
If I ever thought such a thing!
All I know is this:
My wounds opened and bled   4880
Freely, last night, and stained
My bedding, which is why your son
Suspects me, though he has no right to."
And Méléagant replied, .
"By God, the devil and all   4885
The fiends of Hell have betrayed you!
You worked up too much of a sweat,
Last night, and that's why your wounds
Came open, and you bled. There's nothing
You can say to defend yourself: 4890
Blood in both places is the plainest
Proof in the world, and we see it.
A crime so clearly proven
Deserves to be punished. No knight
Of your reputation has ever   4895
Fallen so far: you stand
Before us, covered with shame."
"My lord, my lord," cried Kay
To the king, "I'll defend my lady
And myself against your son's   4900
Accusation! I have no strength,
It may kill me, but he has no right!"
"Combat is out of the question,"
Said the king. "You're too badly hurt."
"Let me fight him, my lord.   4905

Even sick and weak
As I am, I'll meet him in combat
And prove by the blade of my sword
I'm not guilty of this crime!"
But the queen had already, in secret,   4910
Sent for Lancelot,
And told the king she'd produce
A knight who'd defend Sir Kay
Against this accusation,
If Méléagant had the courage.   4915
And Méléagant immediately
Said, "Choose whoever
You like, without exception—
Even a giant!—and I promise
A fight to the death." As he spoke   4920
These words, Lancelot entered,
And so many knights crowded
Into the hall it was filled
To bursting. The moment he appeared
The queen set out the quarrel   4925
For all to hear, young
And old: "Lancelot, this
Is the deeply disgraceful thing
Of which Méléagant has accused me,
And declares he will spread both far   4930
And wide unless you make him
Unsay it. Sir Kay, he claims,
Enjoyed my bed last night,
In proof of which he points
To these curtains, and this bed, both bloodstained.   4935
And he claims the crime will be proven
If Kay, or someone fighting

In his name, can't defend against it."
"You will never need to defend
Yourself, my lady, once
I'm with you. May God in Heaven   4940
Desire no stain on your name.
Whoever thinks this is true
Will have to prove it in combat,
And with me. Whatever strength   4945
I have, I hereby pledge
In your defense. I am ready
For combat." Then Méléagant
Leaped forth. "God save my soul,
That's just what I'd like, I'm more   4950
Than ready and not in the least
Worried!" "Your majesty," said Lancelot,
"As I understand the legal
Requirements of judicial combat
In cases of false accusation,   4955
Such combat can only occur
Under oath." And Méléagant
Instantly answered, with great
Assurance, "Let it be sworn to!
Bring out the holy relics: 4960
I stand with justice and right!"
Lancelot replied at once,
"May God on high help me,
But no one who knows Sir Kay
Could think he had done such a thing."   4965
They called for their horses, their armor
And weapons; their orders were obeyed
As quickly as possible. Squires
Helped them into their armor,

And then the relics were brought.   4970
Méléagant came forward,
And Lancelot right beside him;
Both of them fell to their knees;
And Méléagant stretched out
His hand above the holy   4975
Objects, and swore, loud
And clear: "In the name of God
And these relics, Sir Kay slept
With the queen last night, in her bed,
And took his pleasure." "And I   4980
Swear you're lying," said Lancelot.
"He never came to her bed.
May Our Lord be willing to take
His vengeance on whoever's lying,
And let the truth be known.   4985
But let me swear another
Oath, which is this: no matter
Who it may hurt, or how much,
If I defeat this man
Again, with only the help   4990
Of God and these holy relics
Lying here before us,
I'll offer him no mercy."
And hearing this oath as the knight
Swore it, the king was not happy.   4995
      Once their oaths had been sworn,
Squires led out their horses,
Both of them beautiful beasts,
And each of them mounted, and then
Dashed straight at the other   5000
As fast as their horses could gallop.

The huge beasts collided
With such immense force
That all the knights had left
Of their lances were the handles in their hands.   5005
And both were swept to the ground,
But not like a pair of corpses,
For they jumped quickly to their feet
And began doing as much
Damage as they could with their swords.   5010
Fiery sparks leaped
Toward the sky, from both their helmets.
They pressed their attacks fiercely,
Bare blades clashing, both knights
Constantly moving forward   5015
And back, wielding their swords
As quickly as they could, neither
Taking a quiet breath
Or resting. The sorrowful king
Called up to the queen,   5020
Who'd climbed to a balcony high
In the tower, where she sat and watched,
And asked her, in the name of God,
To stop the combat. "Do
Whatever seems to you best,"   5025
Replied the queen, in good faith.
"I will oppose you in nothing."
Hearing the king's request
Perfectly well, and the answer
Given by the queen, Lancelot   5030
Had no desire to continue;
His furious sword was still.
But Méléagant kept

Attacking, not wanting to be stopped,
So the king stepped between them   5035
And took hold of his son, who swore
That peace was the furthest thing
From his mind: "Let me go on
Fighting!" "Have sense enough
To be quiet and listen," said the king.   5040
"Taking my advice
Will neither shame you nor hurt you.
Things can be done the right way
Or the wrong! Don't you remember
Challenging him to combat   5045
At King Arthur's court? Fighting
There will bring you greater honor,
If you win, than combat anywhere
Else in the world!" The king's
Words were meant to calm him,   5050
If anything could. And at last
He succeeded, and drew them apart.
      Now Lancelot, sorely pressed
To finally find Sir Gawain,
Sought first the king's   5055
Permission to leave, and then
The queen's. Permission granted,
He galloped toward the Sunken Bridge,
Followed by a large troop
Of knights—many of whom,   5060
In truth, he'd rather have seen
Stay where they were. The trip
Was long, and took many days,
But at last they drew near the bridge,
Though still some miles away.   5065

They'd barely come close enough
To see the bridge in the distance,
When a dwarf rode out to meet them,
Mounted on a huge horse
Which he spurred on with blows   5070
From a fierce-looking whip. And as
He approached them, he called out
(According to instructions he'd been given):
"Which of you is Lancelot?
Don't conceal him: I'm on   5075
Your side. Just tell me the truth:
What I need to ask him concerns
You all." Lancelot answered
For himself: "I am the man
You wish to see and speak to."   5080
"Ah Lancelot, noble knight!
Leave these people, if you please.
Come with me, alone,
For I've someplace special to take you.
Let no one follow behind us.   5085
Wait right here. It won't
Be long before we're back!"
Suspecting nothing, the knight
Ordered his men to wait,
And followed after the dwarf—   5090
And those who waited would go on
Waiting, and waiting, and waiting
For the knight's return, for the dwarf
Was not his guide, but his captor.
How sad and confused they were going   5095
To be, waiting in vain,
Not knowing what to do.

They began to believe that the dwarf
Had tricked them—and need you ask
If that knowledge made them happy?   5100
Heavy at heart, they hunted
For the knight, not knowing where
He'd been taken, or how to find him.
They took counsel together, and the wisest
Among them, the story tells us,   5105
Agreed that the sensible thing
Would be to continue on
To the Sunken Bridge, close by,
And then, if they found Sir Gawain
Anywhere in sight, take counsel   5110
With him before they went further.
All agreed on this plan,
Without dissent, and off
They rode toward the Sunken Bridge
And soon reached it, and in fact   5115
Found Gawain, who had fallen
From the bridge into the deep
Water, having lost his balance.
His head kept going under,
Then bobbing back to the surface.   5120
They hurried toward him, and using
Sticks, and branches, and boat hooks,
Brought him ashore, still wearing
His mail shirt, his helmet (worth
Any ten of its kind)   5125
On his head, his iron leggings
Rusty and stained with sweat,
For he'd struggled hard to get there,
And overcome a host

Of dangers and murderous assaults.   5130
His lance, his shield, and his horse
Were waiting on the other bank.
Quickly pulling him out,
They couldn't believe he was still
Alive, but after vomiting   5135
Up the water he'd swallowed,
And lying on the ground, silent,
He began to breathe again
And recovered his voice, and words
They could hear and understand   5140
Were able to flow from his heart,
And he seized the moment, and spoke—
And his very first question for those
Who stood in front of him was whether
There was any news of the queen.   5145
They told him she'd never for a minute
Left King Bademagu's
Protection, for he honored her deeply
And served her well. "Has no one
Come to look for her here?"   5150
Demanded Gawain. To which
They answered, "Oh yes, indeed!"
"Who?" "Lancelot of the Lake,
Who crossed the Bridge of Swords;
And claimed her freedom, and won it,   5155
And for all of us, as well.
But a dwarf has tricked and betrayed us,
A hump-backed, grinning monster,
Sly as a fox, who deceived us
All and carried Lancelot   5160
Off, we don't know where."

"When did this happen?" asked Gawain.
"My lord, it happened today,
Not far from here, as Lancelot
Was leading us to meet you."   5165
"And how did he behave,
After he reached this country?"
So they began to tell him,
And told it all, every
Detail, omitting nothing.   5170
And they told him, too, that the queen
Was awaiting him, and would not
Leave for any reason
In the world, before she'd seen him
Or at least learned where he was.   5175
Then Sir Gawain declared,
"When we leave this bridge, shall we try
To find Lancelot?" But every
One of them thought it better
To return to the queen, for she   5180
Could inquire of the king. They were all
Convinced that Méléagant,
Who hated Sir Lancelot,
Had betrayed and captured the knight.
But wherever the king's son   5185
Held him, once the king
Found out, the knight would be freed:
That was certain. Sir Gawain agreed,
And they set off at once, and rode
So swiftly that soon they approached   5190
The court, where they found the queen
And the king, as well as Sir Kay,
But also the treacherous prince,

Plotter of the vicious deceits
That had caused them all such concern   5195
For Lancelot, and such sorrow.
Victims of foul betrayal,
They arrived in obvious grief.
Nor was the queen delighted
By the news they bore, though she tried   5200
Not to display her sadness,
Behaving as well as she could.
Rejoicing at the sight of Sir Gawain
Was required, and she did her best,
But no matter how well she hid   5205
Her grief, it was not hard
To see. She was torn between sorrow
And relief: her heart hurt
For Lancelot, but in Gawain's presence
All she showed was delight.   5210
Whoever heard that Lancelot
Was gone, betrayed, lost,
Was overwhelmed by sadness.
The king would have known great joy,
Making Sir Gawain welcome   5215
At his court, and coming to know him,
But was so oppressed and sorrowful
At Lancelot's betrayal
That he could not pretend to be cheerful.
And the queen begged and implored him   5220
To search both mountains and valleys
All over his land, from end
To end and border to border,
And so, too, Sir Gawain and Sir Kay.
Indeed, there was no one at court   5225

Who did not urge him to action.
"Allow me to settle this
As I will," said the king. "I need
No urging. I could not be more
Concerned. Your prayers and complaints   5230
Can't move me more than my own
Desires." They bowed, and were silent.
The king's messengers rode
Like the wind, all over his realm,
Wise men, well known and experienced,   5235
Crossing the whole country
In search of some clues, some word.
They cast their net as wide
As they could, but found nothing.
And so they returned, empty-   5240
Handed, to where the knights
Were waiting—Gawain, Kay,
And all the others—who said
That, armed and armored, lances
Ready but at rest, they would hunt him   5245
For themselves. After dinner,
One day, as they gathered in the hall,
Preparing to put on their armor,
Take up their weapons and set off
On their quest, a boy came in   5250
And passed among them, walking
Straight to the queen, whose face
No longer bore the color
Of a rose, pale with grief
For Lancelot, not knowing   5255
How or even where
He was. The boy greeted

Her, and the king beside her,
Then each of the others, including
Kay and my lord Gawain.   5260
He held a letter in his hand,
And gave it to the king, who took it
And ordered a man he trusted
To read it out, for all
To hear—a man who could read   5265
Whatever he saw in front of him.
And he read that Lancelot greeted
The noble king, expressing
His thanks for the favors done him
At the court, and the honor shown him,   5270
And announcing himself forever
Ready to repay what he owed.
And then he declared that his path
Had taken him back to King Arthur's
Court, and that Arthur requested   5275
The queen to return, when she wished,
And also Kay and Sir Gawain.
This letter carried his seal,
And commanded belief, and received it.
And how happy everyone was!   5280
The entire court rejoiced.
And the knights said that the next
Dawn would see them riding
Back to their homes. Which was how
It happened: when morning came   5285
They readied themselves, mounted
Their horses, and rode away.
And the king, as happy as the rest,
Followed them down their road

A long and joyous way.   5290
Indeed, he took them to the borders
Of his land, and safely across,
Then said farewell to the queen,
And afterwards all the others.
And as she left, the wise   5295
And courteous queen graciously
Thanked him for all he'd done,
And warmly embraced him, promising
Honor and affection from both
Herself and her royal husband.   5300
Nothing could have pleased him better.
And Sir Gawain, too, declared him
His friend and his lord, and so did
Sir Kay, and all the others.
And then they rode down the road,   5305
And the king commended them all
To God, and saluted these three,
And then all the rest, and went home.
The queen rode without stopping,
Allowing nothing to delay her,   5310
Nor any of those who rode with her.
And then the news of her coming
Reached King Arthur's court,
And Arthur was delighted, his heart
Happy, rejoicing quite   5315
As much for his nephew's sake,
Convinced that Gawain's courage
Had won back the queen, as well
As Sir Kay, and all the rest.
But it wasn't at all what he thought.   5320
The whole town came out

To greet them, welcome them home;
Noble or peasant, everyone
Shouted the same words:
"Welcome, my lord Gawain,   5325
Who brought us back our queen,
And freed a host of ladies
And crowds of other captives!"
But Gawain answered them all:
"I don't deserve this praise.   5330
Don't waste these words on me,
For I've done nothing to earn them.
Indeed, this honor shames me,
For I came to that country too late,
And lost my chance. But Lancelot   5335
Came in time, and earned
More honor than any knight
Alive." "But where has he gone to,
My lord, for he hasn't come back
With you?" "Where?" said Gawain,   5340
Completely astonished. "To our lord,
King Arthur's court. Isn't he
Here?" "No, by God,
Nowhere in all this land!
Nothing's been heard of him   5345
Since our lady the queen left."
And Gawain suddenly saw
That the letter had not been true,
But false, and a lie, deceiving
And betraying them all. And sorrow   5350
Overwhelmed them again,
As slowly they made their way
To court. As soon as he saw them,

Arthur asked what had happened.
And those who knew were quick   5355
To tell him what Lancelot had done,
Freeing the queen, and the others,
And how the dwarf had tricked him,
Led him off and betrayed him
Into chains. The telling   5360
Of this tale angered Arthur,
Filled his heart with heaviness,
But the flooding joy he felt
On the queen's account silenced
Sorrow in the name of happiness: 5365
Having what he wanted most
In the world, the rest hardly mattered.
    Now while the queen had been
Away (as I've heard it said),
The ladies of Arthur's court   5370
Remaining unmarried and without
Protection assembled in council
And decided, one and all,
They'd like to be married as soon
As possible. And so they decided   5375
To stage a tournament challenge,
The lady of Noauz against
The lady of Pomelegoi.
Nothing would be said of knights
Who lost their battles, but those   5380
Who won, and won well, would be promptly
Chosen as husbands and lovers.
The ladies made sure this news
Was known and heard in neighboring
Lands, and even further,   5385

And they set a far-off day
For the start of this challenge, so as many
Men as possible would come.
Now the queen was due home
Before this distant day   5390
Arrived. And as soon as they knew
She'd come, most of these ladies
Flocked to the court, as fast
As they could, presenting themselves
Before the king, begging   5395
And pleading to be granted the right
To ask for something they wanted.
And he agreed in advance
To give them whatever it was,
Not knowing what they might ask.   5400
And then they told him: they wanted
His permission for the queen
To sit and watch their games.
Never liking to say no, ·
He said she could, if she wished.   5405
Delighted, they hurried off
To find the queen and put
The question to her: "My lady,"
They said, "Please: don't
Take back what the king just gave us."   5410
The queen immediately answered,
"And what was that? Tell me!"
And they said, "If you'd like to watch
Our tournament, he won't
Forbid it or interfere   5415
In any way." And so
She said she would surely take part,

Since he'd given his permission.
And then the ladies sent word
All across the kingdom   5420
That the day the tournament opened
The queen herself would make
Her appearance and watch their games.
This news was sent in every
Direction, far and near,   5425
Traveling to such distant places
That it reached even that kingdom
From which, once, no one
Returned, though now whoever
Chose to could enter and leave   5430
Exactly as they pleased. Traveling
So far abroad, told
And retold, the news reached
One of Méléagant's stewards —
Méléagant, that traitor!   5435
May he burn in the fires of Hell!
This steward was Lancelot's jailer:
Hating the knight with a bitter
Passion, Méléagant
Held him there, locked away.   5440
And hearing the day when those games
Would begin, Lancelot's eyes
Overflowed with tears,
And his heart was filled with sadness.
Seeing the knight's immense   5445
Sorrow, the steward's wife
Arranged to ask him, in secret:
"My lord, in the name of God,"
Said the lady, "tell me the truth.

What could have made you so miserable?   5450
You refuse to drink, or to eat;
You never smile, or laugh.
Trust me, please. Tell me
What could torment you like this?"
"Oh, lady! How can you be   5455
Surprised, seeing my sadness?
I'm sick at heart—indeed!—
For the best people in the world
Are assembling, and I won't be there.
And I know they'll come from far   5460
And wide for this tournament challenge.
Still, if you could find it
In your heart—if God gave you
So noble a soul—if you'd let me
Go there—I tell you, you   5465
Can be sure I'll come right back
And be your prisoner again!"
"Indeed," she said, "I'd certainly
Do it, if it didn't ensure
My ruin and then my death.   5470
I live in such fear of my evil
Lord, Méléagant,
That I don't dare. He'd certainly
Kill my husband, too.
Who wouldn't be afraid?   5475
You know how savage he is!"
"Lady, if you have the slightest
Doubt of my coming back
As soon as the tournament's over,
I'll swear you an oath so solemn   5480
That I couldn't possibly break it:

Nothing in all the world
Will keep me from coming back
The moment the tournament's done!"
"By God!" she said. "On one   5485
Condition, I'll do it." "And that
Condition, lady?" "My lord,
Only if you swear just
As solemn an oath that when
You return I will have your love."   5490
"Lady, I swear I'll give you
Whatever is mine to give."
The lady burst into laughter:
"Which means I get nothing at all!
Someone whose word I trust   5495
Tells me you've long since given
Away all the love
You've got. Still, I won't
Be hard, I'll take whatever
I can, and be glad to have it.   5500
I'll accept the pledge you're willing
To give me, so swear you'll return
And be my prisoner again."
         He did exactly as she asked,
Swearing in the name of our Holy   5505
Church he'd come back without fail.
And the lady brought him her husband's
Arms and armor, all red,
And a marvelous horse, as beautiful,
Stout, and strong as could be.   5510
Up he climbed, and rode off,
Resplendent, his weapons and armor
Brilliant, gleaming bright.

The road to Noauz was a long one,
But he arrived, at last,   5515
And took lodgings outside
The town, where no one so noble
Had ever stayed. It was small
And cramped, but he couldn't let himself
Go where he might be known.   5520
Fine and famous knights
Had flocked to the castle, more
Than even a castle could hold:
So many came on the queen's
Account that it couldn't have lodged   5525
A fifth part of them all.
Seven of every eight
Who had made the journey came
Because of the queen! They took
What shelter they could find, for miles   5530
Around in every direction—
In tents and cabins and huts.
No one had ever seen
So many noble ladies
And girls. Lancelot set   5535
His shield outside the door
Of his lodgings, and then, to rest
From his ride, removed his armor
And lay on the narrow, meager
Bed, with its hard mattress   5540
Covered by heavy canvas.
Not wearing his armor, no weapons
In his hands, he lay on his side.
And as he rested in this wretched
Room, a rascally herald   5545

Came by, dressed in a shirt,
His shoes and coat pledged
Against his drinking debts
At the tavern. Barefoot in the bitter
Wind, he came running along,   5550
And saw the shield and stopped,
Studying it hard, but couldn't
Tell who owned it or might
Have put it in that place. The door
Stood unlocked, so in   5555
He went, and saw Lancelot
Lying on the bed, and knew him
At once, and quickly crossed
Himself. And Lancelot told him
He'd better hold his tongue   5560
And let no one know who had come
Or else he'd be better off
With his eyes ripped out and his neck
Broken. "My lord, you've always
Had my respect," said the herald,   5565
"And you do so now. As long
As I live, I'll never ever
Be guilty of anything likely
To make your lordship angry."
But as soon as he left the house   5570
He ran down the street, crying:
"He'll cut them down to size!
He'll cut them down to size!"
He carried his news all over
The town, and people came running   5575
Out, anxious to know
Who he meant, but he didn't dare tell them,

And went on shouting, over
And over—and he was the first
Ever to use the expression: 5580
"He'll cut them down to size!"
He deserves to be called our teacher,
For we learned how to say this from him.
     And now they began to assemble—
The queen, and all the ladies,   5585
And the knights, and all the others—
And armed men were on every
Hand, wherever you looked.
The tournament site was surrounded
With newly built platforms and benches,   5590
Meant for the queen and the ladies,
And all the young girls. No one
Had ever seen such handsome
Viewing stands, so large
And well made. All the women   5595
Would be there, the next day, along
With the queen, to watch and judge
Who fought well, and who
Did not. The knights assembled
In groups of ten, and twenty,   5600
And twenty more, then thirty,
And eighty, and ninety, and a hundred,
And another hundred, then two hundred
More—so many armed
And unarmed knights, that the combat   5605
Might have started on the spot.
So many spears had been brought
For so many eager knights
There seemed an entire forest

Of lances—and not only lances, 5610
But banners and fluttering pennants.
Every knight was ready
For combat, and none needed
To hunt for willing opponents.
And those who came as horsemen 5615
Were equally anxious to perform.
Meadows and plains, fields
Both ploughed and fallow, were crowded
So full of knights that no one
Could possibly have counted them all. 5620
But as yet the tournament's first
Assembly did not include
Lancelot—though when he came,
And the herald saw him, he could not
Keep himself from shouting, 5625
"Here's the one who'll cut them
Down to size! He's here!"
But when they asked him, "Who is he?"
He refused to tell them a thing.
Yet once Lancelot was there, 5630
And fighting, he was worth twenty
Of the best of them: performing as well
As he did, no one could bother
Watching anyone else.
The Pomelegoi camp included 5635
A bold, courageous knight,
Mounted on a horse that could leap
And run faster than a deer.
He was the king of Ireland's
Son, and fought with grace 5640
And skill. But the unknown knight

Was easily four times more
Appreciated. "Who
Can he be, who's fighting so well?"
Then the queen took aside   5645
A quick-witted, sensible girl,
And said, "Young lady, I have
A message for you to deliver,
In as few words as possible.
Step down from this platform and find   5650
That knight for me—the one
Who's carrying a red shield.
Let no one hear you, and say
I order him to fight badly."
Quickly and quietly, the girl   5655
Did as the queen commanded.
She worked her way to the knight's
Side, and stood as close
As she could, then carefully spoke
So softly that no one nearby   5660
Could hear, "Sir, my lady
The queen sent me to give you
Her order: 'Fight badly.'" Hearing
These words, he said he'd gladly
Obey, for he was entirely   5665
Hers. And then he went chasing
A knight as fast as his horse
Could gallop, and swung, and missed.
And from then till dusk fell
He went on fighting badly,   5670
Purely to please the queen.
And now the knights who came after
Him could catch him, and strike him

Heavy blows, and instead
Of responding he ran away.   5675
The whole rest of that day
He never faced an opponent
Head-on; to save his life
He worked at earning only
Shame, and disgrace, and dishonor,   5680
Acting as if the other
Knights filled him with terror.
And those who'd admired him
At first, began to make him
The butt of laughter and jokes.   5685
And the herald who kept insisting
"He's going to beat them all!"
Sat with a long face,
Listening to insults and jokes:
"Friend, you'd better be quiet: 5690
He won't be cutting anyone
To size. You're wasting your boasts
On him, he isn't worth it."
And some people said, "What happened?
He started out so brave,   5695
And now he's a clumsy coward,
Afraid to attack anyone.
Maybe he did so well,
At first, for sheer lack
Of experience. He swung so hard,   5700
At the start, that no one could stand
Against him. He fought like a madman.
But now he's learned so much
About combat he'll probably leave it
Alone for the rest of his life!   5705

We won't see him again.
He hasn't got the courage:
A fraud, that's what he is."
None of this bothered the queen:
Indeed, she was delighted,   5710
For she knew quite well, though she said
Nothing, this had to be Lancelot.
The rest of that day he played
The role of a coward, till night
Fell, and the combat ended.   5715
When the fighting was done, they began
To discuss the day's results.
The king of Ireland's son
Was sure they had to conclude
His was the best performance,   5720
But he fooled only himself,
For many had done as well.
And still the red knight
Had so caught the attention
Of the noblest and loveliest ladies   5725
And girls that throughout the day
They'd only had eyes for him:
They'd seen how well he did,
At first, as if he were truly
Courageous and strong, and then   5730
Become so rank a coward
He couldn't fight at all—
Someone even the worst
Knight could easily beat.
But everyone agreed to come back   5735
Tomorrow and continue the challenge,
So the girls could see who won

[handwritten margin note: her way of identifying him]

Highest honors, and choose
Those noble knights for their husbands.
And then they disbanded for the day,   5740
And returned to their lodgings, and once
They were there, some began
To chatter and gossip among
Themselves, rehearsing what had happened:
"Where has he gone to, that worst   5745
And most despicable of knights?
He's gone into hiding, but where?
Does anyone know how to find him?
Maybe we'll never see him
Again—so deeply in love   5750
With Cowardice that the world
Has never seen such a weakling!
But he's hardly a fool: a coward's
Life is a hundred thousand
Times as easy as a brave man's.   5755
He lives in absolute comfort
And peace, having kissed Cowardice
And accepted all its rewards.
No one will ever see Courage
Stoop so low as to sit   5760
Beside him at his table. Only
Cowardice comes anywhere near him,
For it finds flowing love
In his heart, always ready
To serve it, delighted to offer it   5765
Honor in return for being
Dishonored." And so they gossiped
Away the night; often
Those who pour their scorn

On others, saying whatever 5770
They please, are worse than those
They despise. But at dawn, the next day,
Every knight took up
The challenge once more, ready
For combat. The queen returned 5775
To her place, and the ladies and girls,
Along with a number of knights
Who carried no weapons—captured
Prisoners, and knights who had taken
The cross—but gave the ladies 5780
Helpful hints about
The battle. They'd say, for example:
"Do you see that shield with a golden
Band? That's Governal
De Roberdic. And the knight 5785
Just behind him, who's blazoned
An eagle and a dragon across
His shield? That's the king
Of Aragon's son, who's come
To win himself as much 5790
Fame and honor as he can.
And the knight fighting nearby,
And fighting extremely well—
With his shield partly green
And partly a deep blue, 5795
With a leopard lying on the green?
That's Ignauré the Greedy,
Who loves ladies, and leaves them.
And that knight with a pair of pheasants,
Beak to beak, on his shield? 5800
That's Coguillant de Mautrec.

And those two—do you see them?—side
By side on their dappled horses,
Brown lions on their golden
Shields? One is Semiramis,   5805
And the other's his friend and companion:
They paint their shields exactly
Alike. And that one, whose shield
Shows us a gate, and a stag
Just passing through it? By God,   5810
That's got to be King Ydier!"
They tried to explain it all:
"That shield was made in Limoges;
That's Piladès who's got it.
He's always looking for a good   5815
Fight and the honor he can win.
That other shield comes
From Toulouse—the harness, too—
That's Kay of Estral. And that one,
Do you see it? It comes from Lyon   5820
On the Rhone: there's never been
A better one made. Taulas
Of the Desert won that reward—
And just see how well he wields it!
And that one, over there,   5825
Is English work, from London:
That pair of swallows looks
Ready to fly away.
But they won't: that shield's taken
Some hefty whacks from Poitevin   5830
Steel! Young Thoas has it."
And on they went, describing
Weapons and armor, and men

They knew well. But the knight they'd learned
To despise was nowhere to be seen,   5835
And since they couldn't see him, they thought
He'd fled in disgrace. But the queen
Was anxious to find him, wherever
He was, and sent a messenger
To hunt him down. No one   5840
Was better suited for the task,
It seemed to her, than the girl
Who'd found him once before.
The queen called her over,
Quickly: "Hurry, girl!   5845
Up on your horse! Go find
The same knight I sent you to
Yesterday. Find him at once;
Let nothing get in your way
Or delay you. And tell him, once   5850
Again; 'Fight badly.'
And then I want you to watch
Him closely, and tell me how
He responds." The girl went
Like the wind: she'd watched him leave,   5855
The day before, carefully
Noting the direction, sure
The queen would send her again.
Up and down the ranks
She rode, until she spied him.   5860
And when she'd told him, discreetly,
To fight badly, once more,
If he wanted to keep the queen's
Love, for the queen so ordered,
He answered, "May it be as she wishes."   5865

The girl left him at once.
Then all the squires and men
At arms began to hoot
And cry: "Just look at that!
Wonder of wonders, the red   5870
Knight's returned — but why?
What on earth is he up to?
No knight in all the world
Is such a disgrace, so worthless.
Cowardice holds him so close   5875
To its heart there's nothing he can do."
The girl hurried back
To the waiting queen, so anxious
To hear his response she would scarcely
Let the messenger catch   5880
Her breath. And having heard it,
The queen could hardly contain
Her joy, for now she knew
Without doubt he was hers, both body
And soul. So she ordered the girl   5885
To hurry back and tell him,
Instead, that he was to fight
As well as he could. And the girl
Agreed to go back at once,
Not stopping to rest. She hurried   5890
Down from the platform, heading
Straight to the groom who held
Her horse's reins, and into
The saddle she climbed, and rode
Back to the knight she'd just left,   5895
And quickly gave him her message:
"My lady directs you, sir,

To fight as well as you can."
"Tell her," he answered, "that whenever
I know what she wants, nothing   5900
Matters to me but her pleasure:
I feel no pain in pleasing
Her." She wasted no time
Bringing this message back
To her mistress, sure that the queen   5905
Would be overjoyed to hear it.
She returned by the shortest possible
Route, directly to the queen,
Equally anxious, who rose
And came toward her, without   5910
However descending down
From the platform. The girl was glad
To climb up, carrying such good
News. Up the steps
She went, and when she drew close   5915
She said, "My lady, I've never
Known so noble a knight—
So utterly happy to obey
Whatever order you give him
That, to tell you the simple   5920
Truth, it's all the same
Whether you want him to excel
Or to play the cowardly fool."
"Indeed," said the queen. "So it seems."
And then she walked back where she'd been   5925
And sat watching the knights.
And Lancelot seized his shield
By the straps, overwhelmingly
Eager, fairly burning

With desire to show his true   5930
Courage. Swinging his horse
Around, he galloped between
The ranks, astonishing those
Who'd spent so much of the night
And the morning mocking and making   5935
Fun of him. Ah,
Such great pleasure they'd had
At his expense! And now
The king of Ireland's son
Took up his shield and his spear   5940
And galloped as fast as he could
Straight at Lancelot.
The crashing shock as they came
Together persuaded the king
Of Ireland's son he'd had   5945
Enough, for his spear splintered
Apart, not having struck
Dry moss but tempered wood.
And as they met, Lancelot
Taught him a little trick,   5950
Pinning his arm behind
His shield, and against his body,
And forcing him out of his saddle.
And knights came dashing up
From all directions, ready   5955
To fight on both sides,
For and against Lancelot.
Some fought for their lords,
And some for themselves, trying
To win what honor they could,   5960
But all that long day Gawain,

Though he was there, never
Took up arms on either
Side, delighted simply
To watch the exploits of the knight   5965
In red, who seemed to his knowing
Eyes to eclipse everyone
Else on the field: next
To him, they vanished from sight!
And the rascally herald recovered   5970
His voice, and shouted out loud:
"He's cutting them down to size!
Now you'll see what he'll do!
Now he'll show you what he's worth!"
Then Lancelot turned his horse,   5975
Heading straight for a singularly
Elegant knight and striking
So hard that he hurled him to the ground
At least a hundred feet
Away. Wielding sword   5980
And spear alike, he fought
So well that whoever was not
Engaged in combat was delighted
To watch him, and even many
In the middle of the battle were dazzled,   5985
Thrilled to see how he tumbled
Knights to the ground, and their horses
Falling with them. Hardly
Anyone stayed in the saddle!
And having won so many   5990
Horses, he freely gave them
Away. And those who had mocked him
Said, "We're shamed unto death!

What a terrible wrong we committed,
Scorning such a man,   5995
For surely he's worth a thousand
Of anyone out on that field!
No living, breathing knight
Could possibly be his equal;
They're worthless, compared to him."   6000
And all the unmarried ladies
And girls, amazed at the wonders
He performed, exclaimed that he'd stop them
From marrying, for how could they count
On their wealth, their beauty, their rank   6005
And status, or their noble breeding,
To capture so perfect a knight,
For whom their beauty and wealth
Would be worth nothing? Just
The same, many among them   6010
Silently vowed not
To accept anyone as their lord
And master, not this year:
If they could not have him in marriage,
They'd settle for no one else!   6015
And hearing what high honor
They dreamed of, the queen smiled
To herself, and mocked them. She knew
That even if they brought all
The gold in Arabia, and set it   6020
Before him, he (for whom
They all longed) would not
Take the best, most beautiful,
Most noble among them. But every
One of them wanted him,   6025

Each as jealous of the other
As if they already had him,
For it seemed to them only right:
There might be men who could please them,
But no one else, they were sure,   6030
Could possibly do what they'd seen him
Doing. When the tournament ended,
All who had fought on either
Side could say with conviction
That no one was a match for the knight   6035
In red. They were all agreed,
And were right. But as he rode off
He let his shield fall
Where he saw the crowd was thickest,
And his spear, and his saddlecloth,   6040
And then he galloped away.
Stripped of all colors and markings
He made his escape, no one
Even aware he was gone.
And then he hurried along   6045
The road, heading directly
Back where he'd come from, determined
To keep his promise. The tournament
Over, everyone sought him,
Wondering where he was,   6050
But he'd left them without a clue,
Not waiting to be recognized.
The remaining knights were deeply
Upset: they'd happily
Have showered him with honors.   6055
But sad as the knights might be,
Unable to find him, the young

Unmarried women, when they heard
He was gone, were even more
Unhappy, and swore by Saint John   6060
There'd be no marriages
That year: if they couldn't have
The one they wanted, they'd have
No one at all. The challenge
Had been taken, but none of the knights!   6065
And Lancelot hurried on,
Returning swiftly to his prison.
But the lady's husband came back
Some days before him, and at once
Asked after the knight.   6070
And the lady, having given
Her husband's armor to the knight,
And his fine sword and spear,
And his horse, beautifully harnessed,
Confessed the whole truth,   6075
Telling her husband she'd let
The knight go to Noauz,
To fight in the tournament there.
"Lady, you couldn't have done worse,"
Said her husband. "Indeed you couldn't!   6080
This will bring me terrible
Trouble, for Méléagant,
My lord, will treat me more harshly
Than any shipwrecked sailor.
As soon as he finds out,   6085
I'm ruined and as good as dead;
He'll have no pity on me."
"Good husband, don't be afraid,"
Said the lady. "There's nothing to be

Afraid of, nothing at all.   6090
The knight will return as swiftly
As he can, exactly as he swore
He would, in the name of the holy
Saints." But her husband leaped
On his horse and hurried to his lord,   6095
And told him the entire story.
When Méléagant heard
How Lancelot had sworn
To the lady he'd return to his prison,
He felt vastly relieved.   6100
"He won't break that oath,"
He said. "I know he won't.
But all the same I'm exceedingly
Angry at what your wife
Has done. I'd infinitely rather   6105
He hadn't been to the tournament.
Ride to the road he'll come back on,
And this time make sure he's locked up
So tight he can't ever
Get out. Let him enjoy   6110
No freedom whatever. Then come
And tell me it's been done." "Exactly
As you say," said the steward, and hurried
Off. He found Lancelot
Had returned to his house and once   6115
Again was his prisoner, and quickly
Sent a messenger to his lord
By the shortest and most direct
Of routes, so Méléagant
Would know the knight had come back.   6120
And hearing this news, the prince

Commanded carpenters and masons—
The best craftsmen in the land—
And ordered them, whether they liked it
Or not, to set to work   6125
At once, and without the slightest
Delay build him a tower,
Not stopping till it was done.
They carried stones from the seashore,
For Gorre lay close to a great   6130
Arm of the sea, and its coast
Was long. And Méléagant
Knew of an island in that sea.
And he ordered timber and stones
Brought there, and the tower built.   6135
In fewer than fifty-seven
Days it was done, a tall
Tower with thick walls.
And when it was finished, in the darkness
Of night he had Lancelot taken   6140
To the tower and locked in,
And he ordered the doors walled up,
And made the masons swear
That as long as they lived they'd never
Say that such a tower   6145
Existed.* And thus he meant
To keep his secret, allowing
No exit or entry but a tiny
Window. And there Lancelot

the end.

* At approximately this point, for reasons we do not know, Chrétien
abandoned the poem, which was finished (as we are told in line 7111) by
"Godfroiz de Leigni, li clers" (Godfrey of Lagny, a learned cleric)

Was forced to live, not fed   6150
Much, or well, or often,
And only through the little
Window, all according
To careful instructions given
By that criminal, Méléagant.   6155
And since whatever the prince
Wanted had been done, he rode
Directly to King Arthur's court,
And the moment he got there came
Swaggering before the king,   6160
Drunk with pride and disorder,
And began to state his case:
"King, I'm sworn to combat,
Here in front of you
And your court. But I can't find   6165
My opponent, Lancelot.   oho!
Never mind: I've come,
As I must, to make this public
Announcement, with all of you present.
And if he's here, let him   6170
Make himself known, and swear
To meet me a year from today.
I've no way of knowing if you've
Been told how this combat
Came about, but I see,   6175
Here in your court, a good many
Knights who were there, and surely
They can tell you what they know,
If they're willing to speak the truth.
But if he denies it, there'll be   6180
No need for me to hire

A champion: I'll fight for myself."
The queen, who was seated beside
Her husband, drew herself closer
And began to speak, but softly: 6185
"My lord, do you know who this is?
It's Méléagant, who kidnapped
Me, when Sir Kay was my escort.
He's guilty of shameful things."
And the king answered her,   6190
"My lady, I understood
As much, and I also know
He held many of my people."
The queen said nothing more,
And the king addressed himself   6195
To Méléagant: "As God
Is my witness, my friend, we know
Nothing of Lancelot,
And deeply regret that fact."
"My lord," said Méléagant,   6200
"Lancelot told me I would surely
Find him here. This battle
Must take place at your court
And nowhere else. Let all
Your assembled barons hear   6205
My words: I summon that knight
To make his appearance before you,
According to the terms we agreed on,
In exactly a year from today."
        And then Sir Gawain rose   6210
To his feet, pierced to the heart
By the words he'd heard, and said,
"My lord, in all this land

No one has news of Lancelot.
But we'll go on looking, and in   6215
A year, if God is willing,
We'll have found him, unless
He's dead or held a prisoner.
But if he doesn't appear,
My lord, let me assume   6220
This challenge, and fight in his name
On the day that's been set." "Aha!
By God," said Méléagant,
"Let him do it, good lord!
He wants to, and I agree,   6225
For in all the world there's no one
I'd rather meet in combat,
Except for Lancelot himself.
But understand me well:
I'll fight one or the other   6230
But no one else. No one!"
And the king agreed: either
Lancelot or Gawain,
If Lancelot never appeared.
And then Méléagant left   6235
King Arthur's court, and rode
Until he reached the court
Of King Bademagu, his father.
And to show his father how very
Fierce and brave he was,   6240
He carefully composed his face
In ways wonderful to behold.
That day, in his city of Bath,
The king had held a joyous
Court, it being his birthday   6245

And a time for celebration.
    And he'd brought to Bath a host
Of knights, and ladies, and many
Others: the palace hall
Was filled to overflowing.   6250
But among the young ladies was one
I want to tell you, in advance,
You'll soon be hearing more of,
And this was Méléagant's sister.
But I can't tell you now,   6255
Or else I'll mix up my story
And get it all out of order,
And I don't want to spoil it
Or bend it out of its path,
But follow it straight and clear.*   6260
So let me tell you simply
This: Méléagant came
To the court, and in front of them all,
Knights and ladies and servants,
Announced, as loud as he could,   6265
"Father, may God save you!
Now tell me truly, if you please,
How happy and proud one should be,
What honor one must deserve,
To have shaken King Arthur's court!"   6270
Not waiting for the rest of the story,
The king replied, "My son,
All those who are truly good

* "Cette lourde intervention [This heavy-handed intrusion]," as Daniel
Poirion observes, may well be a sign of the substitute-poet's anxiety to
stay on course

Ought to be honored and served
Exactly as they each deserve,   6275
And we should seek their company."
And then, to flatter the prince,
He asked him not to be silent
But to say what had happened, where
He had come from, and what he wanted.   6280
"My lord," said his son, "by any
Chance can you recall
The details of that agreement
With Sir Lancelot, duly
Made and recorded, and reached   6285
With your assistance? I'm sure
You do remember, of course,
That in front of a number of knights
It was agreed we'd meet in combat
At King Arthur's court, a year   6290
From that day. I came there, as I should,
Armed and equipped and ready
Exactly as agreed: in short,
Whatever I had to do,
I did. I called for Lancelot,   6295
The opponent I'd come to fight,
But neither saw nor met him.
He's disappeared, run off.
Before I left, Gawain
Pledged that if Lancelot   6300
Is no longer alive, or for any
Reason doesn't appear
In time, there'll be no need
For another postponement, for he
Himself will undertake   6305

To fight in Lancelot's name.
No one at King Arthur's court
Has a better reputation.
But before the elder trees blossom
Again, we'll see if he   6310
Deserves it—and as for me,
I wish that day were tomorrow."
"My son," said his father, "right now
You talk like an utter fool!
Every word you say   6315
Reveals what a fool you are:
Truly, a good heart
Shows itself humble, but a fool's
Pride can't be concealed.
I tell you these things, my son,   6320
Because your heart is too hard
And dry for sweetness or friendship;
It has no room for compassion;
It burns with raging folly.
That's what ruins your judgment;   6325
And that's what causes you trouble.
If you're brave, those
Who know it will say so whenever
It needs to be said. A man
Of courage won't bother with words   6330
That make himself look better.
Facts are enough: praising
Yourself won't add a feather
To your glory. Indeed, it makes you
Worth less. I scold you—and why   6335
Do I bother? A fool won't listen.
Trying to lift a fool

From his folly is a waste of time.
Surely, one can offer
The ripest wisdom in the world,   6340
But it's worthless, unless it's used,
And floats away with the wind."
Then Méléagant went out
Of his head with rage. Let me
Tell you plainly: no man   6345
Born of woman has ever
Been seen so wild, so blazing
With anger—and in his fury
He cut away all ties
With his father, not trying to soften   6350
Matters, but saying, instead:
"And are you dreaming—or delirious—
Saying I'm a fool
For telling you just what happened?
I came to you as one comes   6355
To his lord, to his father, but you
Apparently see things differently,
Insulting me in the grossest
Terms. That's villainous—vile!
How can you possibly explain   6360
Taking such a tone with me?"
"But I can." "And how—how?"
"All I can see in you,
My son, is rage and anger.
I know your furious heart,   6365
And I know the harm it will do you.
What kind of fool could believe
That Lancelot, famous for chivalry,
Is so afraid of you

That he'd run away and hide?   6370
He'd have to be dead—or perhaps
Shut so tightly in prison,
Set behind such doors,
That he has no freedom to leave.
And if he's dead, or been   6375
So badly mistreated, no anger
Will be greater than mine. Ah,
What a loss it would be
If such a man, of immense
Merit, so handsome, so brave,   6380
So wise, has died so young!
God keep it from being true."
And then the king was silent.
But everything he'd said
Had been heard, and understood,   6385
By one of his daughters, only
A girl—but precisely the girl
I spoke of before. She
Was deeply displeased to hear
Such news of Lancelot.   6390
She was sure he'd been hidden away,
But had no idea where to look.
"May I lose my place in Heaven,"
She vowed, "if I let myself rest
Before I find some way   6395
To learn for sure just where
He is." And without a moment's
Delay, not making a sound,
She ran and jumped on a mild,
Sweet-tempered mule—but I have   6400
To admit that, once she'd left

Her father's court, she hadn't
The faintest idea what direction
To take. Neither knowing nor asking,
She headed the mule along   6405
The very first road she found,
Riding completely by chance,
With no servants or knights to help her.
She rode as fast as she could,
Desperate to get where she wanted   6410
To go. For a long time,
Though she rode hard, she found
Nothing. But she could not rest,
Nor stay long in any
Place, if she ever expected   6415
To accomplish what she meant to do,
Which was to free Lancelot—
If she could find him, and if
She could free him. But still, I suspect
She had to hunt in many   6420
Lands, and hunt, and hunt,
Before she heard any news.
But why should I waste your time,
Telling you all the details?
For more than a month she rode   6425
Up hill and down, mounting
And remounting her mule, and never
Learning anything more
Than she'd known before she started.
All her traveling had taken her   6430
Nowhere. And then one day
As she crossed a meadow, sadly,
Slowly, she saw in the distance,

Along the coast, a tower.
But why a tower, without   6435
A single house nearby?
It was, of course, the tower
Her brother had built as a prison
For Lancelot, but she didn't know it.
But the moment she saw it, she couldn't   6440
Turn her eyes away,
But stared, and thought, and thought.
And somehow her heart told her
That this was what she had searched for:
Just when she'd given up hope,   6445
Fortune, which had let her labor
So long, had shown her the way.
        So the girl rode toward the tower,
And finally got there. Then she rode
Around and around it, listening   6450
As carefully as she possibly could,
Trying to find some clue
That would lighten her heart.
She studied that tower from top
To bottom, and from side to side,   6455
Astonished to find a structure
So large without any doors
Or windows, with a single, tiny
Exception. Stoutly built,
And tall, it had neither stairs   6460
Nor ladders. It was meant as a prison,
And Lancelot was surely inside!
Before she'd let herself eat
She had to know the truth!
She thought of calling his name,   6465

But before the word could be spoken
She stopped herself, and stood
Silent, hearing a voice
From inside those strange walls
Crying a loud complaint   6470
And asking only for death.
It craved and hungered for death,
For life was too full of sorrow:
Enough of living! enough
Of this body! he cried feebly,   6475
His voice hoarse and low.
"Oh Fortune! How cruelly your wheel
Has turned against me! You've swung me
Upside down, off
The heights and into the valley.   6480
What once went well, goes badly;
You weep for me, though you used
To laugh. Ah, miserable wretch!
How could you trust her, who leaves you
Like this? How long did it take her   6485
To tumble you down from glory?
Oh Fortune, how badly you've tricked me!
And yet, why should you care?
What does anything mean
To you? Oh Holy Cross,   6490
Oh Holy Spirit! I'm lost
—Annihilated!—It's the end
Of everything. But oh,
You great Gawain! Unmatched
For your goodness, how can it be   6495
You haven't come to help me!
You're taking too long: this

Is not what courtliness
Requires. You were my friend:
You should have come to my aid.   6500
I swear, and I know it's true,
I'd have hunted on every shore
Of the sea, and in hidden places,
And I'd have gone on hunting
For seven years, or ten,   6505
If I knew you were held in prison,
Until I finally found you.
But why do I go on complaining?
You didn't think enough
Of me to take the trouble: 6510
Any peasant will tell you
It's hard to find a true friend!
Put a friend to the test
And then you see who truly
Cares. Alas! I've been locked   6515
In this tower for more than a year.
Oh Gawain, what a mistake—
How wrong to leave me here!
But perhaps, perhaps you don't know,
And maybe I'm wrong to blame you.   6520
Yes—that's right—I remember:
What wicked thoughts I think,
Knowing as I do that nothing
Anywhere on earth could keep
You and your people from coming   6525
To pull me out of this pit,
This misery, if only
You'd known the truth. And you'd come
Driven by love and affection,

For haven't we always been comrades?   6530
How could I see it differently?
But what's the point? It won't happen.
May he be cursed by God
And Saint Sylvester, eternally
Damned, he who brought this   6535
On me! This Méléagant
Is the foulest fiend alive,
Impelled by the blackest hatred."
And then the calm of exhaustion
Fell on the sufferer, and he said   6540
No more. But she who listened
From down below had heard
Everything, nor did she stay
Silent, for she sensed success.
Choosing her words with care,   6545
She called, as loud as she could:
"Lancelot! My friend, you
Up there, speak to your friend."
But Lancelot did not hear her.
So she called out louder still,   6550
And even enfeebled as he was
This time he heard, and wondered
Who it could possibly be.
He heard a voice, and it called
His name—but who could it be?   6555
He thought it must be a ghost.
Looking all around him
He saw no one; there was no one
There. He could see himself,
And the tower. "Lord: what   6560
Am I hearing? There's no one—but I hear

Someone. It must be a miracle.
I'm not asleep. I'm awake.
Perhaps I was just sleeping
And heard this voice in a dream.   6565
But now I'm awake, and I'm sorry."
Then he struggled to his feet
And little by little made
His way to the tiny window,
And leaned against the wall,   6570
And looked in every direction,
And, peering out as best
He could, suddenly saw
The person who'd called his name.
He didn't know her, but he saw her.   6575
Yet she knew him at once,
And said, "Lancelot, I've come
A long, long way to find you.
And now, thank God, I've finally
Succeeded, now I've found you.   6580
I was the one, as you rode
Toward the Bridge of Swords, who asked you
To grant me a wish, and you did,
Most cheerfully. Recall:
I asked for the head of the knight   6585
You conquered, and you cut if off.
He was not someone I loved.
I've gone to all this trouble
Because you granted that wish.
That's why you see me here."   6590
"Young lady," the prisoner replied,
"I thank you most profoundly.
If I can escape from this place

I'll be more than generously rewarded
For whatever service you were rendered.   6595
And if you can get me out
I swear I'll be yours to command
For all the rest of my life:
I swear it by the apostle Paul.
And as I expect to see   6600
Our Lord, there'll never be a day
When I won't do what you ask.
Whatever you ask, if it's in
My power, will be done—and done
As quickly as I can do it."   6605
"Have no doubt, my friend:
You're about to be freed from your prison.
This day will see your deliverance:
I wouldn't abandon your rescue
For a thousand pounds in gold!   6610
And after you're free, I'll help you
To a long, comforting rest.
Whatever you ask of me
Will be yours, if it gives you pleasure.
And nothing will make you ill   6615
At ease. But first I need
To find, wherever I can,
A device to widen this tiny
Window so you can pass through."
"May God help you find it!"   6620
Said Lancelot, with great fervor.
"I have a coil of rope
Which my keepers gave me to draw up
My food—chunks of hard
Barley bread and muddy   6625

Water, which sickened me, body
And soul." Then Bademagu's
Daughter found a short,
Sharp, heavy ax
And brought it to Lancelot,   6630
Who banged and hammered and smashed
At the wall until, though it wasn't
Easy, he'd made himself
An opening more than wide
Enough. How overjoyed   6635
He was, finding himself
Free of his prison, able
To leave the cage he'd been locked in!
He was free—he could go where he pleased!
And understand me: even   6640
Had he been offered all
The gold in the world if only
He'd go back in—all of it,
All his, free and clear—
He'd never turn and go back.   6645
        So now the knight was free,
But so exceedingly feeble
And weak that he tottered when he tried
To walk. So she gently set him
Up on the mule, and sat   6650
Behind him, and they hurried away.
But she carefully followed a different
Road, so no one would see them—
A circuitous, cautious path
Instead of the open highway.   6655
She knew they'd be in trouble,
If anyone saw their faces—

Exactly what she did not want!
And thus, by avoiding dangerous
Places, she brought them to a favorite   6660
Retreat, where she often stayed:
A quiet, lovely spot.
The house and all its servants
Were completely hers to command;
Whatever she could want was there   6665
In abundance, safe and secluded.
Lancelot came there with her,
And as soon as he reached the house
They removed his filthy clothing
And the girl put him to sleep   6670
In a tall, magnificent bed,
And later gave him a bath
And such wonderful care that I couldn't
Tell you half if I tried:
She treated him as sweetly   6675
As if he'd been her father.
She brought him back to life,
Completely renewed and restored,
With the grace and beauty of an angel
Instead of a shaggy tramp.   6680
He was strong, he was handsome, and he left
His bed. And the girl gave him
The finest robes she could find,
And helped him put them on.
He wore them, as happy and light   6685
Of heart as a bird on the wing.
He hugged and kissed the girl,
Then said, with great affection:
"My dear, only you

And God deserve to be thanked   6690
For making me healthy again.
You led me out of my prison,
And so my heart, my body,
My service, and all I own,
Are yours to do with as you will.   6695
You've done so much for me
That I'm yours. And yet, how long
I've been away from King Arthur's
Court—my lord, who's freely
Given me honors. There's much   6700
I need to do. Sweet noble
Friend, I beg you in the name
Of affection to let me go there,
As I gladly would, if you pleased."
"Lancelot, my dear,"   6705
Said the girl, "of course you should go.
The only things I long for
Are goodness and honor for you."
She owned a marvelous horse,
The best ever seen by man,   6710
And she gave it as a gift, and he mounted
At once, not needing the stirrups—
Up he went, like a flash!
They freely commended each other
To God, who deceives no one.   6715
        And Lancelot went on his way
So happy that nothing I could tell you,
No matter how hard I tried,
Could express the infinite joy
He carried in his heart, finally   6720
Freed from the jail he'd been in.

But he also said to himself,
Over and over, that the corrupt
Traitor who'd tricked him into
Prison would pay for his treachery: 6725
"I escaped in spite of him!"
And he swore on the body and soul
Of the earth's Creator that even
All the wealth of the world
From Babylon to Ghent   6730
Wouldn't buy Méléagant's life,
If he beat him in battle once more:
He'd committed too many crimes.
And as it happened, Lancelot
Would soon have the chance to make good   6735
On the threats he was making, for that
Same day this Méléagant
Appeared at King Arthur's court
Of his own accord, not waiting
For an invitation. And the moment   6740
He got there, he insisted on seeing
Sir Gawain at once. And that evil
Prince asked about Lancelot,
Pretending ignorance and calling
Him a wicked traitor,   6745
A cowardly rascal no one
Could find! But in fact he knew
A good deal less than he thought!
Gawain told him the truth:
Lancelot had not been seen.   6750
"Since you, at least, have appeared,"
Said Méléagant, "fulfill
The pledge you gave me. I can't

Wait any longer." And Gawain
Answered, "I'll honor it just   6755
As soon as I can, if God,
In whom I trust, is willing.
I expect to come off well
In this combat, and if the game
Is won, in the name of God   6760
And Saint Fides,* as I think it will be,
Be warned that I mean to win
It all. I will not stop."
And not delaying a moment,
He ordered a rug unrolled   6765
On the ground in front of him. And at once,
In perfect sequence, his squires
Attended to all his commands,
Without a grumble or complaint,
Setting to work with a will.   6770
They got the rug and unrolled it
Exactly as he'd ordered. Quickly,
He settled himself in place
And instructed the squires (who'd shed
Their cloaks for the task) to begin   6775
The process of making him ready
For combat. There were three of them—
His cousins, perhaps, or his nephews—
All experts with arms and armor:
The work was performed so well,   6780
With such practiced, knowing hands,
That no one in all the world
Could have quarreled with a single thing

* Fides of Agen, patron saint of the monastery of Conques

Lancelot becomes less honorable because
it is suggested that he will still
sleep with her, still betray his lord

They did, or done it better.
And when he was ready, two of them   6785
Brought in a Spanish stallion—
Faster on level ground,
In woods, up hills, down valleys,
Than Bucephalus himself.
And then the illustrious Gawain,   6790
Most perfect in chivalry of any
Christian knight, mounted
And rode the horse I've described.
And just as he reached for his shield
He suddenly saw, right   6795
In front of him, Lancelot dismounting.
Gawain thought it miraculous,
This sudden, unexpected
Appearance—so strange, indeed,
That he couldn't have been more astonished   6800
Had the skies opened and dropped
Lancelot down in front of him!
But once he saw it was truly
His friend, there was nothing in all
The world that needed doing   6805
More than climbing right down
And running to Lancelot, arms
Extended, hugging and kissing
His friend. What pleasure, what joy
To find his long-lost comrade!   6810
And let me tell you—and you'd better
Believe me—if they had chosen
Gawain king, but on condition
Lancelot be lost again,
Then Gawain would have said no.   6815

And then the king learned
That Lancelot had finally returned
And was safe and sound, and everyone
Else heard (though not all
Were pleased). But Arthur's court   6820
Rejoiced almost as one,
For they'd waited a very long time.
Every courtier, high
And low, old and young,
Was delighted. Where sorrow had prevailed,   6825
Happiness took its place.
Sadness fled, and pleasure
And celebration came.
Was the queen there to share it?
Indeed she was, most of all.   6830
And how? My God, where else
Would she be? Had she ever been happier
Than his coming made her? Could she keep
Herself from running to greet him?
And how she ran! She hugged him   6835
So hard that her body came dangerously
Close to risking everything
And following where her heart led.
But what did her heart dictate?
Kisses and other delights.   6840
Then why did the body hold back?
Could her joy have been more complete?
Was there any disgust or dislike?
Certainly not, not a bit.
But she had good reason for restraint: 6845
The king was there, and others,
Watching with wide-open eyes,

And she might have given it all
Away, had she done, in front
Of them all, what her heart longed for.   6850
If Reason hadn't restrained
The wild passion she felt,
The world would have known her feelings,
Which would have been folly indeed.
Which was why she held back her heart   6855
And locked wild passion away:
Reason led her to wait,
To reconsider, to watch   *negates the*
For a better time and place,
Something a good deal more private, *tragedy*   6860
When the wind would be blowing clear
And strong for a better harbor.
The king showered honors
On Lancelot, and rejoiced, and then
He said, "My friend, how long   6865
It's been since news of any
Living man pleased me
So much. But I must inquire:
Where have you been? What country,
What place, could have held you so long?   6870
For one whole winter and summer
I've looked for you, up and down,
And never heard a thing."
"Your majesty," said Lancelot,
"I can tell you the story in very   6875
Few words, just as it happened.
When your people were freed from his prison,
Méléagant, that foul
Traitor, shamefully tricked me

And took me captive, and from that 6880
Moment on held me prisoner
In a tower at the edge of the sea.
He had me sealed inside,
And I'd be in that misery still
Except for the help of a friend, 6885
A girl for whom, once,
I did some small service.
I reaped a rich reward,
High honors and great
Goodness, for so small a favor! 6890
But that man for whom I've no
Affection, who brought me so much
Evil and misery and shame,
I'd like to settle accounts
With him as quickly as I can. 6895
He's come here, wanting his payment,
And he'll get it! Why wait to give him
Exactly what he's owed? And I,
My lord, am more than ready:
God forbid he'll enjoy it!" 6900
Then Gawain said to Lancelot,
"My friend, since I owe you so much,
And it's hardly a costly matter,
Let me make this payment for you.
I'm already armored, and mounted, 6905
And ready, as you see. My dear
Sweet friend, don't deny me
This favor, which I'd love to perform."
But Lancelot said he'd give up
An eye, or even two, 6910
Before he'd permit it. It could

Not happen, he swore: this
Was a debt he owed, and he'd pay it,
Just as he'd sworn he would.
And Gawain saw that no matter   6915
What he said, he couldn't
Prevail: he pulled the mail shirt
Off his back and completely
Disarmed. Quickly, quietly
Lancelot made himself ready: 6920
This was a debt he could hardly
Wait to settle. His heart
Would be heavy until Méléagant
Had been paid. And the treacherous prince
Could scarcely believe his eyes,   6925
Seeing what he saw: he was almost
Out of his mind, unable
To control his thoughts. "What a fool
I was," he said, "not
To be sure he was still safely   6930
Locked in my prison, my tower,
Before I came here, for now
He's about to turn on me.
But why, oh God, should I
Have gone? What could have made me   6935
Think he'd ever escape?
Weren't the walls thick
And strong, the tower tall?
Where was there a crack
He could have gotten through,   6940
Except with help from outside?
Did someone reveal the secret?
Suppose the walls fell down,

The entire tower collapsed?
He'd surely have been killed, crushed,   6945
Cut to pieces. By God,
Of course he would—completely!
Without a doubt he'd be dead.
But before those walls collapsed,
I think the seas would have dried   6950
To the very last drop, and the end
Of the world would have come—unless
Something broke them down.
But that wasn't what happened:
Someone had to have helped him,   6955
He couldn't have done it alone.
Someone's plotted against me.
But however he did it, he escaped.
I could have kept it from happening,
Had I been more careful; he'd never   6960
Have reappeared at this court.
And now it's too late for regrets.
The peasants tell the truth,
In their good old proverb: once
The horse is out of the stable   6965
It's too late to lock the door.
And now I'll have to deal
With shame, and insults, and pain;
I'll experience more than enough!
But why do I need to suffer?   6970
As long as I'm still alive
I can give as good as I get,
If God, in whom I trust,
So wishes." He took what comfort
He could, wanting only   6975

To meet his enemy in combat.
He wouldn't wait long, I think,
For Lancelot, who fully expected
To kill him, was anxiously seeking him
Out. But before the battle,   6980
The king dispatched them both
To a valley below his castle —
Ireland held nothing more beautiful.
So down they went, as quickly
As their horses would take them. And the king   6985
Came, too, and everyone else,
An immense crowd, all of them
Hurrying to witness this combat.
There were knights watching from windows,
Along with flocks of beautiful,   6990
Noblewomen and girls.
           A sycamore towered in that valley,
As lovely a tree as existed;
There was plenty of room; in every
Season of the year, fresh   6995
And beautiful grass grew
All around it. This sycamore dated
From the days of Abel; and at
Its foot there ran a sparkling,
Quick-flowing stream, coursing   7000
Along a bed of gravel
So clear that it gleamed like silver.
The water drained away,
I believe, through a pipe of pure gold,
Passing across the fields   7005
And into a valley between
Two trees. And here the king

Was pleased to seat himself;
Nothing could have suited him better.
He had his people draw back   7010
Behind him. And Lancelot quickly
Charged at Méléagant
Like a man transported by hate.
But before he struck a single
Blow, he shouted fiercely,   7015
"Hear my formal challenge!
And know that, no matter what comes,
Nothing will make me spare you!"
And spurring his horse, he drew back
About as far as the length   7020
Of a bow shot, and then they rushed
At one another as fast
As horses could carry them, shields
Clashing so sharply together
That even well-crafted wood   7025
Was cut and cracked, though neither
Man was wounded: not yet.
They turned, rode back, and charged
Again, once more clashing
As hard as they could against   7030
Their strong and well-made shields,
Each of them summoning all
His strength, for each was a valiant
Knight, full of courage
And mounted on a strong and quick-footed   7035
Horse. Each of them smashed
Mighty blows on the other's
Shield, for their spears did not break,
But pierced through the wood, straight

To the bare flesh. Pushing   7040
With all their strength, each
Succeeded in knocking the other
Out of his saddle. In spite of
Breastplates, saddle girths,
And spurs, both knights tumbled   7045
Backwards off their horses
And fell to the bare earth.
Freed of their riders, the excited
Animals galloped off,
Still biting and kicking at each other,   7050
Each trying to maim and kill.
And the fallen knights jumped
To their feet as fast as they could,
Quickly drawing their swords,
The steel engraved with their names.   7055
Holding the blades high,
To protect their faces, they slashed
And probed, hunting some opening
For sharp steel to push through.
Lancelot was supremely confident,   7060
Knowing himself to be twice
As good a swordsman, having
Studied the art since childhood.
They struck huge blows on the shields
Still hung from their necks, and on   7065
The hammered gold on their helmets,
Each of them swinging fiercely,
But Lancelot, pressing him hard,
Found an opening under
His shield and cut so sharp   7070
And quick that, in spite of the iron

Protecting the arm, he cut it
Clean through. Knowing he was lost,
Méléagant resolved
To sell his severed right arm   7075
As dearly as he could, taking
Any chance he might have.
Drowning in pain and despair,
He was nearly out of his head;
Nothing mattered any more   7080
But hurting Lancelot in return.
He leaped forward, hoping
To surprise him, but Lancelot was ready,
Fetching him such a blow
With his sharp sword that April   7085
Would come, and May would go by,
And Méléagant wouldn't recover:
He sliced so deep through the nose guard
That three teeth were shattered.
And Méléagant was so wild   7090
With anger he couldn't speak;
Begging for mercy was the last thing
He thought of, folly clutching
His heart far too firmly.
Lancelot approached, unlaced   7095
His helmet, and cut off his head.
He'd never escape again!
He fell to the ground, dead.
And let me assure you, no one
Who was there, watching the battle,   7100
Felt the slightest pity.
The king and his courtiers and ladies
Were fairly jumping for joy.

Then the happiest among them all
Helped Lancelot out of his armor,   7105
And led him away in triumph.
      Gentlemen: if I tried to tell you
More, I'd exceed my charge,
For my task was to finish this tale.
So here this story stops.   7110
Godfrey of Lagny, a learned
Cleric, has ended this romance.
Let no one criticize me
For completing what Chrétien began,
For Chrétien himself was willing   7115
To let me accomplish the task.
I began where the tower walled up
Lancelot and went on from there
To the end. Nothing else
Was added, and nothing was changed,   7120
To keep from ruining the story.

What . . .

Afterword

Joseph J. Duggan

Chrétien begins *Lancelot: The Knight of the Cart* in a manner untypical of his earlier romances, with a statement of his indebtedness to a patron, Marie, countess of Champagne. Marie, who was the daughter of King Louis VII of France and Eleanor of Aquitaine,* had been countess since her marriage to Henry the Liberal in 1164. When her husband died on March 16, 1181, Marie became regent of the county of Champagne on behalf of her son, also named Henry.

The date of composition of *Lancelot* is uncertain, but most specialists place it after 1176 and before 1182, at about the time of *Yvain: The Knight of the Lion*. The court of Champagne had become an active literary center toward which a number of writers and poets gravitated: the lyric poets Conon de Béthune and Gace Brulé (who was Marie's vassal), the spiritual writer Pierre de Celle, Jehan le Venelais, author of the *Venjance Alexandre,* Evrat, who wrote a long verse translation of Genesis into Old French, Guy of Bazoches, author of a universal his-

---

* Louis and Eleanor had been divorced in 1152 and by the time of *Lancelot* she had been married to Henry Plantagenet for almost two decades. Henry became king of England in 1154.

tory that is now lost, and an anonymous poet who produced a
paraphrase of Psalm 44 of the Vulgate Bible, "Eructavit," for
Marie. Count Henry, an educated man, corresponded with John
of Salisbury and other scholars. Gautier of Arras dedicated his
romance *Eracle* to Marie and two other nobles, and her half-
brother King Richard Lion-Heart of England addressed a poem
to her during his captivity. By far the most illustrious author
associated with the court of Champagne, however, was Chrétien
himself, and although his first romance, *Erec and Enide,* was
probably composed for a noble in the Plantagenet orbit and his
second, *Cligès,* may have been as well, Chrétien identified himself with Troyes in Champagne and was now clearly writing for
the Countess Marie, who held her court in that town. Within the
same circle appears to have been Andreas Capellanus (Andrew
the Chaplain), author of a treatise known as the *Art of Courtly
Love,* who appears to have been attached to the royal court of
Philip Augustus, king of France from 1180 and nephew of Count
Henry. It is in this literary context that Chrétien states his debt
to Marie.

But that statement is problematic. First, Chrétien declares
himself to be entirely at the countess's disposal and, after insisting he has no wish to flatter her, flatters her. Yet he does not
seem to want to identify himself wholeheartedly with the task
at hand, preferring to give her commands greater weight in the
enterprise than his own efforts. She gave him the subject and
the meaning to impose on it, whereas he is willing to claim for
himself only the toil involved in writing the work. Is this simply
more flattery, or is Chrétien anticipating the need to defend
himself from the accusations of other readers and listeners?

One reason to think that Chrétien is calculating how to distance himself from the romance while also carrying out the
countess's wishes is that *Lancelot* is in essential ways unlike his

other romances. This is true above all on the thematic level. The
love that Lancelot and Guinevere share is consummated in a
scene of adultery that is out of keeping with the depiction of
love in Chrétien's other works, including love between a young
man and a married woman in the romance that is thought directly to precede this one, *Cligès*. There Fenice, married to
the emperor of Constantinople, takes great pains, including
allowing herself briefly to be buried alive, to avoid acquiring
a reputation like that of the adulteress Iseult, renowned in the
literature of the period as the lover of her husband's nephew
Tristan. In *Lancelot*, not only do Guinevere and Lancelot commit adultery, they do it while she is a prisoner of Arthur's enemy
Méléagant, leaving themselves all the more vulnerable to the
whisperings of *lauzengiers*, courtiers who curry favor by passing
on just such gossip to offended husbands. In fact, the woman
who allows Lancelot to leave his prison and take part in the
tournament of Noauz has it on hearsay that he has already fallen
in love (ll. 5495–98), so Chrétien would have us believe that the
relationship was known among the courtiers of Gorre. Before
her abduction, Guinevere says under her breath, but within ear-
shot of one of Arthur's counts, that an unidentified "you," who
can only be Lancelot, would not let her be led off without resistance, an utterance that has no follow-up in the romance and
no meaning unless it is that Chrétien wants his audience to real-
ize that Guinevere's attachment was no secret at Arthur's court
either. Few crimes were more serious than committing adultery
with the wife of one's lord.

In addition, the principal characters in Chrétien's other
romances are motivated above all by the desire to avoid being
shamed. For the male roles, this entails a determination never
to act in a cowardly fashion on the battlefield, whether in war or
in the mock warfare of the tournament. But Lancelot willingly

abases himself in the tournament of Noauz by doing badly at the behest of Guinevere, who uses the command as an identity test. As a result, he misses his blows in the joust, avoids engagements, and attracts the mockery of the crowd. That he finally fights all out after starting the second day's combat poorly at her command is little comfort, since this conduct is also regulated by the queen's whim. Lancelot has thus given himself over entirely into the service of the lady whom he loves, to the detriment of knightly ideals and reputation. Although at first he thinks that Guinevere may be angry at him for climbing into the cart, and logically so, because virtually everyone in Gorre seems to disrespect him for that action, he utters no reproach either when Guinevere initially rejects him or when she finally tells him she was cold to him because he hesitated for two steps before getting into the ignominious vehicle. During that momentary delay, Reason was admonishing him against doing anything that would cause him shame or reproach, while Love asked him to ignore all consideration of shame. In his dealings with the queen, then, Lancelot exhibits *fine amor,* "pure" love, in the sense of being an all-encompassing, exclusive affection, while he continues to remain subject to the restraining effects of shame in his relations with other characters. But Chrétien never openly expresses in *Lancelot* any hesitancy over this deviation from the principles that exemplify praiseworthy conduct in his other works, so where do his true sentiments lie?

An indication of Chrétien's attitude toward the material and its interpretation is found in his treatment of Lancelot's deeds. When Lancelot finally reaches the queen in Gorre after the ordeal of the Sword Bridge, she spurns him because, as he later learns, he hesitated before climbing into the cart. Lancelot, however, is oblivious to this fault early in his quest and single-mindedly pursues his goal of finding her to the point of cutting

a ridiculous figure. In the Castle of the Perilous Bed, so intent is
he on seeing the queen's cortège that he almost falls to his death
from a window, but his companion, Gawain, saves him. In the
encounter at the ford, he forgets his name, whether he is armed,
and where he is going, and in fact loses himself under the in-
fluence of his quest, recovering his senses only when, having
been unhorsed, he feels the cold water of the ford on his back.
At the sight of Guinevere's comb, he almost faints and begins
to adore the strands of hair that cling to it. He fights Méléagant
in a ridiculous stance, turning from him so that he can keep
the queen in his field of view. He ineffectually attempts suicide
by tying himself to his horse's neck. In portraying his hero in
such ways, bereft of all sense of measure in his obsession for a
lover who is also the wife of his lord, Chrétien undercuts both
the character and the import of Lancelot's actions. Even the
situation through which the queen was jeopardized by Arthur's
allowing Kay to defend her is ludicrous, since it is merely a reaction to the seneschal's feigned petulance. Arthur himself, who
fails to step forward in response to Méléagant's opening challenge and liberate the captives from Gorre, and who not only
allows Kay to put the queen in jeopardy but does not even pur-
sue the two until Gawain urges him to do so, is endowed with a
weaker personality than anywhere else in Chrétien's corpus.

Yet another piece of evidence is Chrétien's failure to finish the
romance, giving it over for completion to a certain Godfrey of
Lagny, otherwise unknown to literary history. But how to interpret this clue? Chrétien's final work, *Perceval: The Story of the
Grail,* is also unfinished, but in that case the thirteenth-century
writer Gerbert de Montreuil informs us that Chrétien died before finishing it. Could it be that Chrétien confided the task of
closure to Godfrey because his heart was no longer in it? Did
Marie of Champagne disapprove of Lancelot's love being por-

trayed as a mania? Documentary support for either alternative is, alas, lacking.

Whatever the slant one wishes to put on these aspects of Chrétien's romance, its treatment of the relationship between Lancelot and the queen made it one of the most influential works of the Middle Ages. Guinevere's betrayal of Arthur is the source of the kingdom's decline in the thirteenth-century Lancelot-Grail Cycle of prose romances, also known as the Vulgate Cycle: the *Story of the Holy Grail, Merlin, Lancelot,* the *Quest for the Holy Grail,* and the *Death of King Arthur.* This cycle in turn became a major source for Sir Thomas Malory's *Morte Darthur* and eventually for most of the hundreds of other retellings of the Arthurian legend up to the present. The love scene between Lancelot and Guinevere was analyzed in an article that appeared in the French journal *Romania* in 1883 in which Gaston Paris, the most respected French literary medievalist of the period, formulated the concept "courtly love." That term has since taken on so much conceptual baggage as to have outlived its usefulness in the minds of many, but it was for years the focal point of discussions of medieval erotic theory and practice.

❀

Where did Chrétien or his patron get the tale? Arthur himself is treated as a hero in Welsh verse from an early period, perhaps as far back as the sixth century and certainly from the ninth. In the *Gododdin,* a collection of elegies commemorating the Battle of Catraeth in the year 600 but extant only in a thirteenth-century manuscript, a warrior is praised for his prowess in battle "although he was no Arthur." The eleventh-century *Culhwch and Olwen,* a prose tale in Welsh, presents Arthur as the chief of a warband. Geoffrey of Monmouth's astonishingly successful *History of the Kings of Britain* (ca. 1136), which carries Arthur's renown beyond the confines of Britain, recounts the rebellion of the king's nephew Mordred, who lives in adultery with Guinevere while attempting to usurp the throne. This episode leads to the climactic Battle of Camblam and Arthur's withdrawal to the Isle of Avalon, where his "mortal" wounds are attended to.

Although Geoffrey of Monmouth nowhere mentions Lancelot, he does refer to the magician Bladud, founder of Bath and father of King Leir (Shakespeare's Lear), who learned to fly on manmade wings but fell to his death. The Norman writer Wace repeats the association of the magician Bladud with Bath in his translation of Geoffrey's *History,* entitled *Le Roman de Brut* (*The Romance of Brutus,* ca. 1155), which is likely to have been the immediate source for Chrétien's Bademagu, whose name signifies, after all, "magician of Bath." The earliest trace of this figure in Welsh is as Baedan, father of Maylwyas (equivalent of Melwas), in *Culhwch and Olwen,* but he may be the avatar of a man mentioned in Irish annals under the name Baitán, father of Máel, who participated in the Battle of Degsastan in 603.

The legend of Guinevere's abduction is attested in the lines of "A Conversation Between Arthur and Guinevere," a fragmentary mid-twelfth-century Welsh poem that is difficult to interpret because there is no indication of who is speaking in a given line. What is clear, however, is that Guinevere (in Welsh, Gwenhwyvar, "white phantom") has been abducted by Melwas, lord of the Isle of Glass, and that someone, probably Arthur, who is compared unfavorably to Cei, the Welsh equivalent of Kay, has come to take her back. In the early twelfth-century *Life of Gildas* by Caradog of Llancarfan,

Gildas . . . arrived at Glastonbury, at the time when king Melwas was reigning in the summer country. . . . Glastonbury, that is, the glassy city, which took its name from glass, is a city that had its name originally in the British tongue. It was besieged by the tyrant Arthur with a count-less multitude on account of his wife, Gwenhwyfar, whom the aforesaid wicked king Melwas had violated and carried off, and brought there for protection, owing to the asylum afforded by the city's invulnerable position due to the fortifications of thickets of reed, river, and marsh. The rebellious king, Arthur, had searched for the queen throughout the course of one year, and at last heard that she was staying there. There-upon he roused the armies of Cornwall and Devon; war was prepared between the enemies. When he saw this, the abbot of Glastonbury, attended by the clergy and Gildas the wise, stepped in between the contending armies, and in a peaceable manner advised his king, Mel-was, to restore the ravished lady. Accordingly, she . . . was restored in peace and goodwill. When these things were done, the two kings gave the abbot a gift of many domains.*

The kingdom of Gorre in *Lancelot* represents what Cara-dog of Llancarfan refers to as the "summer country," Somerset, here the area around Glastonbury (Welsh *Ynys Wydrin,* "Isle of Glass"). Linguistically, "Gorre" is the equivalent of *voirre,* an Old French word that means "glass." Glastonbury was asso-ciated with the Arthurian legend, and in fact in 1191, a decade or so after Chrétien composed *Lancelot,* the monks of the abbey of Glastonbury claimed to have discovered there the tomb of Arthur and Guinevere. Caradog's incorporation of the story of Guinevere's abduction in his *Life of Gildas* is obviously a churchman's attempt to appropriate a popular tale for the glory of his subject. His mention of the name of Arthur's queen is the second earliest after a reference in *Culhwch and Olwen.*

Long before this legend became the basis for Chrétien's

* Translation based on Rachel Bromwich, ed. and trans., *Trioedd Ynys Prydein: Triads of the Isle of Britain* (Cardiff: University of Wales Press, 1978), 381–82.

Lancelot, it was the subject of a set of sculptures executed before 1125 on the archivolt of the north portal of the cathedral of Modena. There a series of figures, identified by inscriptions, is shown progressing toward a fortress: Artus of Bretania, Che (Kay), Galvagin (Gawain), Galvariun, and Isdernus (Ydier). In the fortress are Mardoc and Winlogee (a variation on the Breton form of Guinevere's name), defended by Burmaltus and Carrado (Caradoc). The abductor may be Burmaltus, perhaps a "Melwas" figure, as is Chrétien's "Méléagant." Chrétien had mentioned Melwas, lord of the Isle of Glass, in *Erec and Enide* as one of those invited to the eponymous couple's wedding. Breton storytellers had carried a version of the tale of Guinevere's abduction as far as northern Italy, showing that it was widely disseminated in the period.

Conspicuously lacking in the three sources for knowledge of the old version of Guinevere's abduction, however, as well as in the *History of the Kings of Britain,* is Lancelot, who is absent from Welsh tradition before the thirteenth century but, despite his appearance in *Erec and Enide* and *Cligès,* seems not to be a figure of Chrétien's invention. A new element in the story that does seem to come from Chrétien (or from his patron, Countess Marie) is the adultery between Guinevere and one of her husband's knights, a relationship consistently designated a felony in medieval legal sources. Méléagant is technically correct in making the legal charge of adultery against the queen, but Lancelot is able to defeat him in single combat because Méléagant wrongly identified Kay as her partner. According to the theory underlying medieval trial by combat, God would see to it that the victor would be the person who was in the right according to the exact charge that was brought.

In his *Art of Courtly Love* (ca. 1185), whose original title was *De Arte honeste amandi,* literally *On the Art of Loving Honor-*

ably, Andreas Capellanus set forth a number of principles that concord with the behavior of Lancelot and Guinevere in *Lancelot,* roughly contemporary with his treatise. Andreas defines love as "a certain inborn suffering derived from the sight of and excessive meditation upon the beauty of the opposite sex."* Among love's rules as set forth by Andreas are that the lover should keep himself chaste for the sake of his beloved, that he should obey the commands of ladies in all matters and devote himself to the service of love, that love cannot exist within the bonds of matrimony (marriage being a contract and thus not a relationship of free giving), and that love is the source of all good. Andreas illustrates his views of love's workings by presenting twenty-one difficult cases, most of which are judged by great ladies, among them Marie of Champagne and Eleanor of Aquitaine. What surprises, then, is not so much that the ideas found in *Lancelot* were current in the milieu in which it was composed, but that they should have been expressed by Chrétien, whose previous works present a favorable portrayal of love within the married state and whose final romance, *Perceval,* is devoid of the theme of adultery.

A romance about Lancelot and the queen that does not derive from Chrétien, although it postdates his work, since it was composed after 1194, is Ulrich von Zatzikoven's German *Lanzelet,* which the author claims is translated from a French book provided to him by the noble Hugh of Morville. The book must have contained a pre-*Lancelot* version of the abduction of Guinevere. Ulrich recounts how Lanzelet was carried off by a water fairy (compare *Lancelot,* ll. 2350–51) when he was younger than two and was brought up among women until

---

* Andreas is quoted according to the translation of John Jay Parry, *The Art of Courtly Love, by Andreas Capellanus* (New York: Ungar, 1941).

age fifteen. Instructed by a young knight in the arts of chivalry, he thrice comes to castles and kills the lord, only to find
that the lord's daughter or niece has fallen in love with him.
The third of these women, Iblis, becomes his wife. Told that
he is related to Arthur, he goes to the court, where he defends
Queen Ginover against Valerin, a Méléagant figure. Valerin
nevertheless abducts Ginover, but Arthur recovers her with the
assistance of a magician, Malduc (the Mardoc of the Modena
archivolt?). After turning a young woman from a dragon back
into human form by kissing her, Lanzelet returns to Iblis and
lives in contentment with her. The French source available to
Ulrich thus stood between the old myth of the abduction of a
Guinevere sought by Arthur and Chrétien's version, in which
Lancelot frees the queen.

But Lancelot's role in Chrétien's romance is not simply to
serve as the queen's rescuer, lover, and champion. He is the
savior as well of those whom the unrelentingly evil Méléagant
has taken to Gorre from Arthur's kingdom, Logres (equivalent
of *Lloegr,* the Welsh word for England, still in use today, whose
original meaning seems to have been "having a nearby border").* Resonances of this role are present in the cemetery scene
in which only Lancelot is able to raise the tombstone inscribed
as destined for the knight who will free the captives from "a
prison from which no one returns" — that is, Gorre (ll. 1904–
15). This aspect of the tale appears to reflect a myth of salvation
from the land of the dead, where "No one's denied entrance, /
But once they're here, they must stay" (ll. 2106–7).

Lancelot progresses toward Guinevere through a series of
tests that challenge his fidelity to the queen as well as his cour-

---

* Eric Hamp, "*Lloegr:* The Welsh Name for England," *Cambridge
Medieval Celtic Studies* 4 (1982): 85.

age. Before he reaches the kingdom of Gorre, these tests occur
in the presence of a dwarf and of five damsels, mysterious characters who seem already somehow to be aware of the purpose
and course of the hero's journey. Both dwarves and solitary
damsels are stock guiding and controlling figures of Arthurian
narrative. In *Lancelot* two, and perhaps three, of the damsels
are one and the same. Méléagant's sister reveals that she is the
fifth damsel (see ll. 6582–86), who successfully asked Lancelot
for the head of a knight whom she hated, as well as the second
damsel, who met him on the way to the Sword Bridge and asked
for a future favor. The third damsel thinks Lancelot recognizes
her (l. 930) and may well be the same woman. The test of the
Perilous Bed, in which Lancelot survives the Flaming Lance,
plays the same role as the lifting of the tombstone in the cemetery, to identify Lancelot as the savior who will free the captives
from Gorre. The battle with the knight at the ford is a test of
courage and prowess. The trials with the fourth damsel—the
feigned rape and the night spent in her bed—are chastity tests.
Once he enters Gorre, Lancelot encounters the good knight
and his family, navigates the Stony Path, survives an entrapment
through the magic ring his mother gave him, refuses a behead-
ing test reminiscent of the later Middle English romance *Sir
Gawain and the Green Knight,* crosses the Sword Bridge, and
arrives at Bademagu's tower. That his journey has led him into
an Otherworld kingdom can hardly be doubted.

To rescue the queen and the other captives, Lancelot must
then overcome Méléagant, whose methods are not limited
to those sanctioned by codes of courtly behavior. Although
Méléagant is portrayed as a Christian, invoking in conventional
ways his faith and trust in God, he treacherously retains Lancelot in prison while purporting to be puzzled over the hero's

failure to present himself for combat at Arthur's court at the appointed time. Méléagant sins less against religious principles than against the obligations of kinship, however, disappointing his benevolent father, Bademagu, in his headstrong pursuit of cruelty and injustice. In a society in which kinship ties were one of the major forces regulating conduct, it is significant that Méléagant's defeat and death should be rendered possible by the steps his own sister takes to free Lancelot from captivity.

Chrétien has constructed a counterexample to the relationship between Méléagant and his father in the unnamed son and elderly father whom Lancelot meets in a meadow on his way to Gorre (ll. 1655-1833). In the case of this pair, the father argues that the son would be foolhardy to risk himself in combat against such an accomplished knight as Lancelot over a young women with whom he is infatuated. The father, who first resorts to physical restraint, eventually wins the argument when the monk who has viewed the incident of the tombstone reveals that Lancelot is unequaled as a knight. Bademagu's arguments have no such salutary effect on his son, who persists in provoking Lancelot until this course of action results in his own destruction. The amount of attention Chrétien gives to this theme makes one wonder if any incident of contemporary social reality now hidden from our view motivated him to fashion these contrasting pairs of exemplary fathers and sons.

On the moral level, a conflict marks Chrétien's characterization of Lancelot. In the larger social sphere his heroism is unquestioned: he is the liberator of the people of Logres and their queen, who in the Celtic context is not just the king's consort but a figure embodying the principle of sovereignty. Yet in feudal society this role depends on Lancelot's vassalic relationship with King Arthur, a relationship he violates by his adultery with the queen. That scene is rich in sacrilegious imagery: Lancelot adores Guinevere as he would a holy relic, feels the pangs of martyrdom as he leaves her, and bows on exiting as if before an altar. The religion of secular love has taken precedence over what can only be characterized as a superficial Christianity, just as love service has triumphed over the vassal's fidelity to his lord.

Recommended for Further Reading

Medieval Texts

Bromwich, Rachel, ed. and trans. *Trioedd Ynys Prydein; Triads of the Isle of Britain*. Edited with an Introduction, Translation, and Commentary. Cardiff: University of Wales Press, 1978.

Jarman, A. O. H., ed. and trans. Aneirin, *Y Gododdin, Britain's Oldest Heroic Poem*. Welsh Classics, 3. Llandysul: Gomer Press, 1988.

Jones, Gwyn, and Thomas Jones, trans. *The Mabinogion*. Everyman's Library. Revised edition. New York: Dutton; London: Dent, 1974.

Parry, John Jay, trans. *The Art of Courtly Love, by Andreas Capellanus*. Records of Civilization, Sources and Studies, 33. New York: Ungar, 1941.

Raffel, Burton, trans. Chrétien de Troyes, *Cligès*. With an Afterword by Joseph J. Duggan. New Haven and London: Yale University Press, 1997.

———. Chrétien de Troyes, *Erec and Enide*. With an Afterword by Joseph J. Duggan. New Haven and London: Yale University Press, 1997.

———. Chrétien de Troyes, *Yvain: The Knight of the Lion*. With an Afterword by Joseph J. Duggan. New Haven and London: Yale University Press, 1987.

Thorpe, Lewis, trans. Geoffrey of Monmouth, *The History of the Kings of Britain*. Harmondsworth: Penguin Books, 1966.

Critical Studies

Baldwin, John W. *The Language of Sex: Five Voices from Northern France Around 1200.* Chicago: University of Chicago Press, 1994.

Benton, John F. "The Court of Champagne as a Literary Center." In *Culture, Power and Personality in Medieval France,* 3-43. Edited by Thomas N. Bisson. London: Hambledon Press, 1991.

———. "Clio and Venus: A Historical View of Medieval Love." In *Culture, Power and Personality in Medieval France,* 99-121. Edited by Thomas N. Bisson. London: Hambledon Press, 1991.

Burns, E. Jane. *Bodytalk: When Women Speak in Old French Literature.* Philadelphia: University of Pennsylvania Press, 1993.

Cross, Tom Peete, and William Albert Nitze. *Lancelot and Guenevere: A Study on the Origins of Courtly Love.* Chicago: University of Chicago Press, 1930.

Frappier, Jean. *Chrétien de Troyes: The Man and His Work.* Translated by Raymond J. Cormier. Athens: Ohio University Press, 1982.

Kelly, Douglas. *"Sens" and "Conjointure" in the Chevalier de la Charrette.* Studies in French Literature, 2. The Hague: Mouton, 1966.

———. *Chrétien de Troyes: An Analytic Bibliography.* Research Bibliographies and Checklists, 17. London: Grant and Cutler, 1976.

———. *The Art of Medieval French Romance.* Madison: University of Wisconsin Press, 1992.

———. *Medieval French Romance.* Twayne's World Authors Series, 838. New York: Twayne, 1993.

Kelly, Douglas, ed. *The Romances of Chrétien de Troyes: A Symposium.* Edward C. Armstrong Monographs on Medieval Literature, 3. Lexington, Ky.: French Forum, 1985.

Lacy, Norris J. *The Craft of Chrétien de Troyes: An Essay on Narrative Art.* Davis Medieval Texts and Studies, 3. Leiden: Brill, 1980.

Loomis, Roger Sherman. *Arthurian Tradition and Chrétien de Troyes.* New York: Columbia University Press, 1949. Reprint, New York: Octagon Books, 1982.

Maddox, Donald. *The Arthurian Romances of Chrétien de Troyes: Once and Future Fictions.* Cambridge Studies in Medieval Literature, 12. Cambridge: Cambridge University Press, 1991.

Noble, Peter S. *Love and Marriage in Chrétien de Troyes.* Cardiff: University of Wales Press, 1982.

Paris, Gaston. "Le Conte de la Charrette." *Romania* 12 (1883): 459–534.

Patch, Howard Rollin. *The Other World, According to Descriptions in Medieval Literature.* Cambridge: Harvard University Press, 1950.

Topsfield, L. T. *Chrétien de Troyes: A Study of the Arthurian Romances.* Cambridge: Cambridge University Press, 1981.

i think the two endings
have a lot to do with
the role of women in
the poem, specifically
because of Meleganit's
sister being the one
who frees Lancelot
because it breaks
the theme that women
have no rights and
they are completely
at the mercy of men
in this society

What it means to be civilized
- Chivalric code
- Lancelot as ultimate epitome of
  the chivalric code?
  - generosity, courtesy, prowess, loyalty

Courtly love / Fine love

- true love is @ first sight
- love makes you a better person
- women are on a pedestal
  ✳ morally, serve women
- service to the beloved woman
- love involves infinite suffering
- secrecy is necessary
✳ women as something to be won
he is the knight of the cart:
he belongs in prison: 1st ending

the whole poem is a man
serving a woman

Lancelot takes his own
honor in the end - almost
a rejection of Guinevere,
he truly becomes the ultimate knight